TRIBAL DEVELOPMENT OF ENERGY RESOURCES AND THE CREATION OF ENERGY JOBS ON INDIAN LANDS

OVERSIGHT HEARING

BEFORE THE

SUBCOMMITTEE ON INDIAN AND ALASKA NATIVE AFFAIRS

OF THE

COMMITTEE ON NATURAL RESOURCES
U.S. HOUSE OF REPRESENTATIVES

ONE HUNDRED TWELFTH CONGRESS

FIRST SESSION

Friday, April 1, 2011

Serial No. 112-16

Printed for the use of the Committee on Natural Resources

Available via the World Wide Web: http://www.fdsys.gov
or
Committee address: http://naturalresources.house.gov

U.S. GOVERNMENT PRINTING OFFICE

65-506 PDF   WASHINGTON : 2011

For sale by the Superintendent of Documents, U.S. Government Printing Office
Internet: bookstore.gpo.gov   Phone: toll free (866) 512–1800; DC area (202) 512–1800
Fax: (202) 512–2104   Mail: Stop IDCC, Washington, DC 20402–0001

COMMITTEE ON NATURAL RESOURCES

DOC HASTINGS, WA, *Chairman*
EDWARD J. MARKEY, MA, *Ranking Democrat Member*

Don Young, AK
John J. Duncan, Jr., TN
Louie Gohmert, TX
Rob Bishop, UT
Doug Lamborn, CO
Robert J. Wittman, VA
Paul C. Broun, GA
John Fleming, LA
Mike Coffman, CO
Tom McClintock, CA
Glenn Thompson, PA
Jeff Denham, CA
Dan Benishek, MI
David Rivera, FL
Jeff Duncan, SC
Scott R. Tipton, CO
Paul A. Gosar, AZ
Raúl R. Labrador, ID
Kristi L. Noem, SD
Steve Southerland II, FL
Bill Flores, TX
Andy Harris, MD
Jeffrey M. Landry, LA
Charles J. "Chuck" Fleischmann, TN
Jon Runyan, NJ
Bill Johnson, OH

Dale E. Kildee, MI
Peter A. DeFazio, OR
Eni F.H. Faleomavaega, AS
Frank Pallone, Jr., NJ
Grace F. Napolitano, CA
Rush D. Holt, NJ
Raúl M. Grijalva, AZ
Madeleine Z. Bordallo, GU
Jim Costa, CA
Dan Boren, OK
Gregorio Kilili Camacho Sablan, CNMI
Martin Heinrich, NM
Ben Ray Luján, NM
John P. Sarbanes, MD
Betty Sutton, OH
Niki Tsongas, MA
Pedro R. Pierluisi, PR
John Garamendi, CA
Colleen W. Hanabusa, HI
Vacancy

Todd Young, *Chief of Staff*
Lisa Pittman, *Chief Counsel*
Jeffrey Duncan, *Democrat Staff Director*
Rick Healy, *Democrat Chief Counsel*

———

SUBCOMMITTEE ON INDIAN AND ALASKA NATIVE AFFAIRS

DON YOUNG, AK, Chairman
DAN BOREN, OK, Ranking Democrat Member

Tom McClintock, CA
Jeff Denham, CA
Dan Benishek, MI
Paul A. Gosar, AZ
Raúl R. Labrador, ID
Kristi L. Noem, SD
Doc Hastings, WA, *ex officio*

Dale E. Kildee, MI
Eni F.H. Faleomavaega, AS
Ben Ray Luján, NM
Colleen W. Hanabusa, HI
Edward J. Markey, MA, *ex officio*

———

CONTENTS

OVERSIGHT HEARING ON "TRIBAL DEVELOP-MENT OF ENERGY RESOURCES AND THE CREATION OF ENERGY JOBS ON INDIAN LANDS."

Friday, April 1, 2011
U.S. House of Representatives
Subcommittee on Indian and Alaska Native Affairs
Committee on Natural Resources
Washington, D.C.

The Subcommittee met, pursuant to call, at 11:00 a.m. in Room 1324, Longworth House Office Building, Hon. Don Young [Chairman of the Subcommittee] presiding.

Present: Representatives Young, Denham, Gosar, Kildee, Faleomavaega, Pallone, Boren, Luján, and Hanabusa.

STATEMENT OF THE HONORABLE DON YOUNG, A REPRESENTATIVE IN CONGRESS FROM THE STATE OF ALASKA

Mr. YOUNG. The Subcommittee will come to order. As you will notice, it is exactly 11 o'clock, and that is the way that I like to do things. There is a quorum because there are two Members here, Mr. Kildee and myself, and so the Subcommittee on Indian and Alaska Native Affairs has a meeting today to hear testimony on the issue of tribal development of energy resources and the creation of energy jobs on Indian lands.

Under Committee Rule 4[f], opening statements are limited to the Chairman and Ranking Member, or his substitute, so that we can hear from our witnesses more quickly.

However, I ask for unanimous consent to include any other Members' opening statements in the hearing record if submitted to the Clerk by the close of business today. Hearing no objection, so ordered.

He is not here, but when Mr. Pallone comes in, I ask for unanimous consent that he be allowed to join us on the dais. All right. The purpose of the hearing today is to receive testimony from tribal leaders and members about obstacles that are delaying the development of energy and other resources on Indian lands.

With 56 million acres of Indian lands in the lower 48 States, and 44 million acres of Native corporate land in my State of Alaska, Native Americans have an enormous potential to contribute to the energy and security of this country.

As many of our witnesses know, tribal lands are estimated to contain 10 percent of the Nation's conventional and renewable energy resources. This is likely an understatement because Federal geologists are typically very conservative in their assessment of energy resources.

A case in point, when we opened up Prudhoe Bay, it was estimated that we had 7 billion barrels of oil, and we have pumped

17 billion barrels so far in the period of time that it was supposed to have gone dry.

Over 15 million acres of Indian lands with energy resources have not been developed. For instance, the Crow Nation has an estimated 3 percent of the United States coal resources, exceeding 9 billion recoverable tons.

As gas prices continue to soar and unemployment ranks high throughout Indian Country, we should continue to encourage and empower tribes to responsibly develop their energy resources.

However, due to outdated and duplicative Federal regulations and laws, tribes often feel that the Federal Government has treated them unfairly when compared to State and local government.

Regulatory obstacles such as the Bureau of Indian Affairs' approval of Rights of Way, the Bureau of Land Management's approval of Applications for Permits to Drill, and National Environmental Policy Act red tape are unjust to the tribes.

These rules and policies often slow energy development and discourage businesses to invest in tribal lands. However, such laws as the Energy Policy Act of 2005 are a step in the right direction.

More specifically, Title 5 of the Act recognizes the authority of tribal governments to negotiate their own leases. Unfortunately, no tribe has applied for this special authority and this Subcommittee will explore reasons why this measure has not been attractive to tribes.

We need to ensure that Federal environmental laws do not impede energy development in Indian Country. I look forward to working with my colleagues on the Committee and tribes to identify unnecessary laws and regulations, and to write necessary regulations to allow tribes to pursue energy self-determination. I now recognize the late Ranking Member.

Mr. BOREN. Thirty seconds.

Mr. YOUNG. In 30 seconds, you could run three 100-yard dashes.

Mr. BOREN. That is right. I did on the way over here.

Mr. YOUNG. Anyway, Mr. Ranking Member, Mr. Boren, you are recognized for an opening statement.

[The prepared statement of Chairman Young follows:]

Statement of The Honorable Don Young,, Chairman, Subcommittee on Indian and Alaska Native Affairs

The purpose of today's hearing is to receive testimony from tribal leaders and members about obstacles that are delaying the development of energy resources on Indian lands.

With 56 million acres of Indian lands in the Lower 48 States and 44 million acres of Native Corporation lands in my state of Alaska, Native Americans have enormous potential to contribute to the energy security of this country.

As many of our witnesses know, tribal lands are estimated to contain ten percent of the nation's conventional and renewable energy resources.

This is likely an understatement because federal geologists are typically very conservative in their assessments of energy resources.

Over 15 million acres of Indian lands with energy resources have not been developed. For instance, the Crow Nation has an estimated three percent of the United States' coal resources—exceeding 9 billion recoverable tons.

As gas prices continue to soar and unemployment remains high throughout Indian Country, we should continue to encourage and empower tribes to responsibly develop their energy resources.

However, because of outdated or duplicative federal regulations and laws, tribes often feel that the federal government is treating them unfairly when compared to states and local governments.

Regulatory obstacles such as the Bureau of Indian Affairs' approval of Rights of Way, the Bureau of Land Management's approval of Applications for Permit to Drill, and National Environmental Policy Act red tape are unjust to tribes.

These rules and policies often slow energy development and discourage businesses to invest on tribal lands.

However, laws such as the Energy Policy Act of 2005 are a step in the right direction. More specifically, Title 5 of the Act recognizes the authority of tribal governments to negotiate their own leases. Unfortunately, no tribe has applied for this special authority and this subcommittee will explore reasons why this measure has not been attractive to tribes.

We need to ensure that federal environmental laws do not impede energy development in Indian Country. I look forward to working with my colleagues on the Committee and tribes to identify unnecessary laws and regulations, and to write necessary legislation to allow tribes to pursue energy self-determination.

———

STATEMENT OF THE HONORABLE DAN BOREN, A REPRESENTATIVE IN CONGRESS FROM THE STATE OF OKLAHOMA

Mr. BOREN. Thank you, Mr. Chairman. First, I would like to welcome all the witnesses here today. Thank you for sharing with us your successes and your hardships in the development of energy resources and jobs in Indian Country.

This issue has long been an oversight on the part of the Congress. I am pleased to be here today to explore how we can encourage tribal growth. I want to start by saying that thus far the Federal Government has missed opportunities that encourage Indian Country to invest in energy as a means to create jobs and create revenue.

There is an immense amount of untapped potential here to better the lives of our tribal neighbors. By looking at gaming, we can see what tribes with access to fair financial incentives and opportunities for growth can accomplish.

In Oklahoma, tribal enterprises are the third largest employer in our State. The revenue that tribes generate goes directly back into the system to improve education, health care, and the overall standard of living.

According to President Shelly's testimony, the unemployment rate among the Navajo people is 48 percent. There is absolutely no reason why, with such rich natural resources, almost half of the Navajo people should be unemployed.

It is our duty to develop the tools to encourage economic growth in a field that will benefit everyone, and that is energy development. We can do this by examining obstacles and creating solutions.

If the bureaucratic red tape is too thick, how can we ease that burden? If the tax system is structured unfairly, what will create an even playing field? If the Federal Government overlooks the funding responsibilities, how in this time of economic accountability can we meet these needs? What can we do to include Indian Country in our movement to lessen our dependence on foreign oil?

I am a proud supporter of both conventional and renewable energy opportunities. After investing in renewable resources, Oklahoma now harnesses a total of 1,130 megawatts of energy from wind farms. I am a sponsor of the NAT GAS Act, which provides incentives to significantly expand the infrastructure necessary to grow the market for natural gas-fueled vehicles.

This bill has a specific provision to extend these incentives to Indian Country. Aside from financial incentives, we can help tribes by ensuring that they have access to proper training and education.

A large part of the overall development process will be increasing the expertise to better handle the complexities of these energy projects. Tribes need access to top-of-the-line training facilities and educational programs, so that they cannot only develop energy resources, but also become leaders in the field.

And finally I wanted to explore the environmental impact of expansion. As an avid outdoorsman, I understand the importance of our country's natural resources. I want to ensure that we act responsibly and grow sustainably.

The EPA, within its jurisdiction, should regulate the industry to protect the environment, while allowing for maximum growth. Permits and paperwork are an inherent part of the process, but tribes on the basis of their tribal affiliation alone should have no more difficulty than the private sector.

I know that the Administration is currently working with tribes to redefine regulations, and I applaud its efforts. I look forward to hearing from our panelists today and working with the Committee in the future on creating these much-needed opportunities.

Again, I thank you for your participation. I also, Mr. Chairman, have some testimony from the Chairman of the Quapaw Nation, and with unanimous consent, I would like to enter that into the record.

Mr. YOUNG. Without objection, so ordered. I thank the gentlemen, Mr. Boren, for that statement.

[The prepared statement of Mr. Boren follows:]

Statement of The Honorable Dan Boren, a Representative in Congress from the State of Oklahoma

Thank you Mr. Chairman.

First I would like to welcome all of the witnesses here today. Thank you for sharing with us your successes and hardships in development of energy resources and jobs in Indian Country. This issue has long been an oversight on the part of Congress. I'm pleased to be here today to explore how we can encourage tribal growth.

I want to start by saying that thus far, the federal government has missed opportunities that encourage Indian Country to invest in energy as a means to create jobs and generate revenue. There is an immense amount of untapped potential here to better the lives of our tribal neighbors.

By looking at gaming, we can see what tribes, with access to fair financial incentive and the opportunity for growth, can accomplish. In Oklahoma, tribal enterprises are the third-largest employer in the state. The revenue tribes generate goes directly back into the system, improving education, health care, and the overall standard of living.

According to President Shelly's testimony, the unemployment rate among the Navajo people is 48 percent. There is absolutely no reason why, with such rich natural resources, almost half the Navajo people should be unemployed.

It is our duty to develop the tools to encourage economic growth in a field that will benefit everyone: energy development.

We can do this by examining obstacles and creating solutions.

If the bureaucratic red tape is too thick, how can we ease that burden? If the tax system is structured unfairly, what will create an even playing field? If the federal government overlooks the funding responsibilities, how, in this time of economic accountability, can we meet these needs? What can we do to include Indian Country in our movement to lessen dependence on foreign oil?

I am a proud supporter of both conventional and renewable energy opportunities. After investing in renewable sources, Oklahoma now harness a total of 1,130 megawatts of energy from wind farms alone.

I am a sponsor of the NAT GAS Act, which provides incentives to significantly expand the infrastructure necessary to grow the market for natural gas fueled vehicles.

This bill has a specific provision to extend these incentives to Indian Country.

Aside from financial incentives, we can help tribes by ensuring they have access to proper training and education. A large part of the overall developmental process will be increasing the expertise to better handle complexities of energy projects.

Tribes need access to top-of-the-line training facilities and educational programs so that they cannot only develop energy resources, but become leaders in the field.

Finally, I want to explore the environmental impact of expansion. As an avid outdoorsman, I understand the importance of our country's natural resources. I want to ensure that we act responsibly and grow sustainably. The EPA should, within its jurisdiction, regulate the industry to protect the environment while allowing for the maximum growth.

Permits and paperwork are an inherent part of the process, but tribes, on the basis of their tribal affiliation alone, should have no more difficulty than the private sector.

I know the administration is currently working with tribes to redefine regulations and I applaud its efforts. I look forward to hearing from our panelists today and working with the committee in the future on creating these much needed opportunities. Again, thank you for your participation today, and I yield the balance of my time.

[The statement of the Quapaw Tribe of Oklahoma submitted for the record by Mr. Boren follows:]

Statement submitted for the record by The Honorable John L. Berrey, Chairman, Tribal Business Committee, Quapaw Tribe of Oklahoma (O–Gah-Pah)

Chairman Young, Ranking Member Boren, and members of the Subcommittee, I am John Berrey and I am the Chairman of the Quapaw Tribe of Oklahoma (O–Gah-Pah).

On behalf of the tribe, I submit the following statement and recommendations for your consideration.

While the Quapaw Tribe is not an energy resource tribe, the tribe has considered a variety of energy development-related projects including a gas-fired electricity plant to be located on Quapaw lands. As a consumer of electricity and other energy resources and byproducts like home heating oil and gasoline, the Quapaw Tribe and its members have a strong interest in seeing that the United States do what is necessary to foster development of all American resources whether they are located on or off Indian reservations.

I want to thank Chairman Young and Ranking Member Boren for holding this hearing because natural and energy resource development holds enormous potential to rehabilitate tribal economies and bring jobs and incomes to Indian people around the country.

The U.S. Departments of Energy and Interior have inventoried both conventional and renewable energy resources owned by and available to Indian tribes and, if these resources were developed, literally trillions of dollars in revenues would flow to the tribes and their members.

One need only look to the success of the Southern Ute Indian Tribe in Colorado, which in twenty years has gone from a passive royalty collector to a natural gas phenomenon generating 1% of all natural gas consumed by Americans.

Despite the potential of Indian energy, the fact is that a maze of uneconomic and outdated Federal laws and regulations and new fees to drill for oil and gas, combined with the ability of states to tax energy projects on Indian lands, and near-limitless challenges to energy projects by environmental groups, significantly erodes the competitiveness of energy development on Indian lands when compared to projects on state and private lands.

Last year we celebrated the 40th anniversary of President Nixon's Special Message to Congress on Indian Affairs in which he articulated Indian Self Determination as the best hope to strengthen tribal governments and rehabilitate tribal economies. Over four decades, Indian tribes have made enormous strides in practicing good governance and re-structuring their governmental systems. With this in mind, it is time for the Federal government to acknowledge these developments and to tailor Federal laws, regulations and policies so that Indian tribes, not Federal officials, make the decisions that will determine whether and under what circumstances tribal energy and other natural resources will be developed.

In 2010, the U.S. Department of the Interior's Office of Indian Energy and Economic Development commissioned the Quapaw Tribe to draft the "Indian Tribal Energy Development Primer" to assist interested Indian tribes and potential partners with the fundamentals of devising, structuring and operating energy projects on Indian tribal lands. I commend that document to the Subcommittee as it continues its review of the challenges to Indian energy development.

As the Subcommittee proceeds to identify and rectify the impediments to Indian tribal energy development, be assured you may call on the Quapaw Tribe to assist in these noble efforts.

Thank you.

———

Mr. YOUNG. We will now hear from our first panel, Secretary Scott Russell, Chairman Tex Hall, and President Ben Shelly, but at this time I also recognize the gentleman from Arizona, Mr, Gosar, for the purpose of introducing the President of the Navajo Nation. Mr. Gosar.

STATEMENT OF THE HONORABLE PAUL GOSAR, A REPRESENTATIVE IN CONGRESS FROM THE STATE OF ARIZONA

Dr. GOSAR. Thank you, Mr. Chairman, and thank you for inviting President Shelly of the Navajo Nation to testify during this important hearing on the obstacles that Indian tribes face in developing energy resources.

I had the pleasure of visiting Window Rock, Arizona, the capital of the Navajo Nation, in January during my townhall tour. I was so warmly received by President Shelly and the members of the Navajo Council, and the community leaders who braved the freezing Window Rock cold, to meet with me and share with me their stories.

I am so hopeful that President Shelly's administration will bring forth a new era of self-determination and economic development. I look forward to his continued leadership and welcome him to the Committee today.

[The prepared statement of Mr. Gosar follows:]

Statement of The Honorable Paul Gosar, a Representative in Congress from the State of Arizona

Chairman Young and Ranking Member Boren, thank you for holding this important hearing today. Not only am I very glad to see my distinguished constituent, President Shelly of the Navajo Nation, but I couldn't be more in support of the idea of bringing tribal leaders to Washington to talk about the challenges they face in developing their energy resources. At a time when gas prices are over $4.00 a gallon in some areas of the country, crippling middle class families and deepening the recession, we must pursue an all of the above energy policy. It is essential for our national security, to create high paying American jobs, and to ease the pain for consumers under the pressure of rising prices. And I can think of few places where economic development is needed more than the Indian reservations. Most tribes in Arizona have unemployment rates approaching or exceeding 50%. 75% of homes in America that lack electricity are located on the Navajo reservation alone. In addition, many Navajo reservation homes lack basic amenities that we take for granted: 31% lack standard plumbing, 28% do not have modern cooking facilities, 32% are without electricity, and 60% cannot even install a landline telephone.

And "all of the above" energy policy cannot proceed without including Indian Country. Tribal lands are estimated to contain 10% of the nation's energy resources, both traditional and renewable. In speaking with my Native American constituents, it is clear to me that Indian Country stands ready to be part of the solution, tapping into coal, gas, oil, wind, and solar power right in their own backyard in order to provide state of the art, low cost energy to their neighboring communities and states.

And yet, as we hold this hearing today, much of Indian Country's energy remains unused.

I believe, and I think today's witnesses will agree, that the federal government is placing roadblocks all throughout tribal lands that are figuratively strangling the tribes, sticking projects in a bureaucratic sinkhole, some never to be seen again. The Indian energy sector is working with both hands tied behind their backs, as they face not only the federal roadblocks that the private sector does, but also need to tangle with BIA for funding and grants.

In Arizona's First District, the Navajo Nation is working on three sites for utility-scaled wind generation development—but environmental mandates are holding up the projects. The Navajo Generating Station (NGS) provides over 500 high paying jobs worth $150 million to tribal members, and the power generated by NGS and delivered to the Central Arizona Project (CAP) provides 45% of Phoenix's water supply and over 80% of Tucson's supply. Yet an EPA rule threatens to make it cost prohibitive to keep the plant operating.

Desert Rock Energy Project is a clean coal plant, operated in conjunction with the Navajo Nation. Desert Rock stands ready to power a large Southwestern corridor from Tucson, Arizona all the way to Las Vegas. The EPA issued a permit in 2008, but yet rescinded the permit in 2009. While Desert Rock waits for EPA to decide its fate, thousands of high paying construction and engineering jobs hang in the balance. We have seen far too much testimony, and far too much evidence, of the EPA imposing extreme demands that are not consistent with Congressional intent and serve only to delay, obstruct and hinder worthwhile projects.

On the Navajo reservation alone, three sites are actively being explored by the tribal utility office for wind turbines, yet the Fish and Wildlife Service (FWS) has ignored the consensus of stakeholders and wrote a nonsensical, out of touch set of rules for wind turbine operations that is leaving these wind projects stagnant.

These delays are not only devastating to Indian Country, and contrary to the promise we made decades ago to allow tribal self determination, but also part of a troubling pattern of Washington control over the West. I am so proud to live in a state with awe inspiring landmarks, beautiful forests, and abundant mineral supply—yet so dismayed at the out of touch and uninformed bureaucrats who dictate to us how we are allowed to use these resources. We in the West know how to form community consensus around the best use of our wild lands and mineral resources, and only ask one thing of Washington in return: get out of the way and allow us to make these responsible decisions.

Again, it is apparent to me that Indian Country stands ready to be part of the solution to our pressing energy crisis. The question is, do federal agencies stand ready to listen, to engage, to cooperate, and mainly to get out of the way of safe domestic energy production?

Thank you. I look forward to the witnesses' testimony and answers.

———

Mr. LUJÁN. Mr. Chairman?

Mr. YOUNG. Yes, sir?

Mr. LUJÁN. If the gentleman would yield quickly.

Dr. GOSAR. I would be happy to.

Mr. LUJÁN. And as well, Mr. Chairman, if it would be all right, I would like to welcome the President of the Navajo Nation, who is New Mexican, as well as Navajo, and Mr. Chairman, Yá'át'ééh, Shik'is, welcome. I look very forward to the testimony today and see how we can better work together to make sure that we are all more respectful to sovereignty and to our Tribal Nations. Thank you, Mr. Chairman.

Mr. YOUNG. I thank the gentleman. A great introduction. The witnesses' written testimony will appear in full in the hearing record, and so I will ask you to keep your oral statements to five minutes as outlined in our invitation letter to you, and under Committee Rule 4[a].

So at this time, I will call, I believe, my first witness. Scott Russell will be the first one up. Mr. Scott Russell, Secretary of the Crow Tribe of Indians.

8

STATEMENT OF SCOTT RUSSELL, SECRETARY, CROW TRIBE EXECUTIVE BRANCH

Mr. RUSSELL. Thank you, Mr. Chairman. I thank you for this opportunity to address this Committee. In 1868, the Crow Nation, with the Fort Laramie treaty, encompassed a reservation of 38 million acres. Through time, we have lost a majority of that reservation, and now we have 2.2 million acres.

And under those 2.2 million acres now lies three percent of the United States' coal reserves. Coal is the primary source of income for our tribe. Two-thirds of our income comes from this. We have been in the coal game for 37 years.

We have some problems that need to be addressed today. There are three different pieces of legislation that can be fixed. The Indian Coal Tax Production Credit; we ask for some form of a vehicle to make this permanent.

When you are in the game of coal the market fluctuates so much that we need something secure so that we are able to plan and invest for the future. Right now if you look at the accelerated depreciation, you also have the employment tax credit. Those need to be incorporated in some form of legislation in the near future.

For our Coal-to-Liquids project, we are looking at close to 2,000 jobs. We are looking at making coal into jet fuel and diesel fuel. We are looking at 900 permanent jobs once this starts.

Our reservation is similar to those of all reservations, which suffer from high unemployment rates. With this Coal-to-Liquids project, we would be able to produce up to 50,000 barrels of oil for clean jet and diesel fuel.

With this, we would need your support in obtaining Department of Defense contracts so that we would be able to help our own. We also have an abundance of other resources, one of which is natural gas.

But it is pretty hard for us to drill. We have to go through a process where there is an application for a permit to drill, and it is a travesty of the system. It started out with $4,000 in costs on it, but now it is up to $6,500 per test well.

And I said it was a travesty to the system. If you walk one step off the reservation, it only costs a hundred dollars. We are set up for failure and with that, we need some legislation.

Now, another process that hinders our productivity is the BIA process. You know, some of these permitting and the red tape that tribes have to go through could take years, and it is really hard for us.

We also have renewable energy. For the Crow Tribe, we have monitors in place throughout our reservation, and it measures close to five and six classification, which is fairly good.

A normal wind farm only needs 3 to 4 classification, and so we are sitting pretty good on that, and most recently, we just passed the Crow Water Rights Sullivan Act of 2010. In that there is a provision to provide money for a hydro facility on our reservation.

We also have a dam there, the Yellowtail Dam. Fifty years ago, 5,500 acres of Crow land was condemned to build this dam, and it produces a half-a-billion kilowatt hours per year.

Up to date the government has made 600 million dollars off this dam on our land, and we have not received any monies from that.

We are at war right now, and in times of war, Native Americans are the highest percentage of any minority group in this country to enlist.

We volunteer, and we fight side-by-side, and right now we are spending billions of dollars overseas in Iraq and Afghanistan. Most recently, we spent more billions of dollars bombing Libya.

It is about time that some of those billions of dollars are returned to help economic development and help rebuild Native America. We are not here for a handout. We are here to partner with these United States and reduce our dependence on foreign oil.

Mr. Chairman, I know that our time is very limited, but I wanted to bring up some of these points, and in my written testimony, it is more in-depth, but I really want to thank you for revitalizing this Committee. It is long overdue.

Fifteen years is a long time, and for that, Mr. Chairman, and Members of the Committee, I thank you for this time.

[The prepared statement of Mr. Russell follows:]

Statement of Scott Russell, Secretary, Crow Nation's Executive Branch, Crow Tribe of Montana

I. Introduction

Good Morning Mr. Chairman and Members of the Natural Resources Committee. Thank you for the opportunity to share the views and concerns of the Crow Nation on Indian energy. The Crow Nation's energy resources are abundant and the financial stability of our Tribe is wholly dependent upon them. The Crow Nation is uniquely positioned to contribute to the energy independence of our country.

We applaud this Committee's leadership in reviewing the vast energy opportunities in Indian Country and the economic value of such resources not only to the Tribes that own them, but to the nation as a whole. Eliminating obstacles to energy project development, along with providing incentives to create jobs in Indian Country to produce energy resources, will build additional national capacity to create even more jobs in the national economy. This is an opportunity that cannot be missed.

In this testimony, I will describe the extent of the Crow Nation's coal, oil and natural gas, and wind energy resources and the existing and planned facilities and projects utilizing these resources. I will also discuss the obstacles to increasing the development of these resources and the solutions we propose to reduce the obstacles. With an estimated 3% of the nation's coal resources, as well as with preliminary estimates of significant oil, natural gas, and wind reserves, the Crow Nation is well positioned to provide the secure and dependable domestic energy resources that our national economy needs. And our energy resources will provide good jobs as we further develop them.

II. Crow Energy Resources

Land and Population

The Crow Nation is a sovereign government located in southeastern Montana. The Crow Nation has three formal treaties with the federal government, concluding with the Fort Laramie Treaty of May 7, 1868. The Crow Reservation originally encompassed most of Wyoming (including the Powder River Basin) and southeastern Montana. Through a series of treaties, agreements and unilateral federal laws over a 70 year span, Crow territory was reduced by 92% to its current 2.2 million acre area.

In addition to this substantial land loss, the remaining tribal land base within the exterior boundary of the Crow Reservation was carved up by the 1920 Crow Allotment Act. In 1919, prior to the Allotment Act, there were already 2,453 allotments, consisting of 482,584 acres. By 1935, there were 5,507 allotments, consisting of 2,054,055 acres (218,136 acres were alienated from tribal ownership by 1935). The Big Horn and Pryor Mountains were not allotted and still remain reserved for the Crow Nation and its citizens.

According to more recent Bureau of Land Management Reports, the land statistics have shifted: 45% Crow allotments; 20% Crow Nation trust land; and 35% non-Indian fee land. In sum, the pattern of surface ownership generally is "checkerboard" with interspersed Crow Nation trust and fee lands, Crow allotments (held in trust for individual Tribal member owners), and non-Indian fee lands. The statistics show limited success of the Crow Nation in reacquiring lost lands, but the reality is a much larger pattern of continued loss.

Today, there are nearly 13,000 enrolled citizens of the Crow Nation, with approximately 8,000 of those residing within the exterior boundaries of the Reservation. Additionally, a recent study indicates that the tribal population will exceed 20,000 citizens by 2015, which will add further stress to our fragile developing economy, and sharply increase the level of basic human services needed by our population. Our goal is to invite more of our citizens to return home to live and resume tribal relations, but we must be able to offer tribal members solid opportunities to hold stable and meaningful employment, homes, and educational opportunities. Our current unemployment rate is 47%. The Crow Nation has always emphasized higher education and we currently have more than 400 annual applications for higher education assistance. Because of federal funding limitations and internal budget constraints, however, we can only fund 90 students each year.

In addition to providing financial support for education, we have a separately chartered tribal college (Little Bighorn College, "LBHC") that started operations in 1981. LBHC has graduated over 300 students to date. LBHC graduates are employed on and around the Crow Reservation in a variety of positions including teachers' aides, computer technicians, office managers and administrative assistants. At least sixty have completed bachelor's degrees and are pursuing professions in education, social work, human services, science, nursing, technology, accounting and business. As we move forward in developing our energy resources, our own college can help to provide our citizens with training in new fields for expanded job opportunities, including vocational-technical courses to support energy development.

Minerals, Past and Present

The Crow Nation has an opportunity to develop tribal resources because the 1920 Crow Allotment Act, as amended in 1968, reserved all minerals, oil and gas on any lands allotted under that Act for the benefit of the entire tribe in perpetuity. Today, although some checkerboarding of mineral rights also exists on the Crow Reservation, subsurface mineral acres are owned primarily by the Crow Nation. For example, in the southeast corner of the Reservation, 1.3 billion tons of recoverable coal are wholly owned by the Nation. The larger portion of natural resources within the Reservation boundaries are recognized but remain largely untapped.

The Crow Nation has developed a limited amount of its resources, typically with royalty (and some tax) revenue received as the lessor. Although the Crow Nation pursued some oil and gas development between the 1920s and 1950s, more recent natural gas development has been hampered by lack of pipeline infrastructure and the Federal Application for Permit to Drill (APD) fee. Most of our governmental revenue is derived from our 38-year relationship with Westmoreland Resources, Inc. Over that period, the Absaloka mine has produced about 150 millions tons of coal and is the largest private employer within the Crow Reservation.

The Crow Nation has very substantial undeveloped mineral resources. It is estimated that we own 3% of the nation's coal resource, exceeding 9 billion recoverable tons. We have been exploring our oil and gas reserves, and preliminary estimates indicate that they are significant. In addition, we have large deposits of industrial minerals, such as limestone and bentonite. Finally, preliminary data suggests that we have class 5/6 wind energy as well as other renewable resources. The Nation is currently in talks with various companies regarding the development of these untapped resources, but barriers have slowed or prohibited significant progress.

III. Crow Energy Projects

A. Absaloka Mine

The Absaloka Mine, owned and operated by Westmoreland Resources Inc. (WRI), is a 15,000-acre single pit surface coal mine complex located near Hardin, Montana and the Crow Indian Reservation. WRI mines coal leased from the Crow Nation pursuant to two different coal leases. The mine shipped its first coal in 1974, and has been a steady and reliable source of coal to its customers, and revenue to the Crow Nation for a continuous 37 year period. The Absaloka Mine was expressly developed to supply Powder River Basin coal to a group of Midwestern utilities, including Xcel Energy's Sherburne County Station near Minneapolis, Minnesota. The mine also enjoys a proximity advantage to these customers relative to its main competitors. Over the years, it has also sold coal to several other upper Midwest utilities as well. Coal is shipped via a 38-mile rail spur to the main line of the Burlington Northern Santa Fe Railroad near Hysham, Montana. WRI is currently evaluating a substantial investment in the construction of a westward bound railroad connection to facilitate coal transportation to explore west coast and export coal sales opportunities.

The Absaloka Mine can produce up to approximately 7.5 million tons of coal annually, and has produced over 172.6 millions of tons over its life. WRI annually pays substantial production taxes and coal royalties to the Crow Nation; $9.9 million of taxes and $9.1 million of royalties were paid in 2010. These fees and taxes amounted to 23% of the gross revenue on the mine last year. These taxes and royalties are representative of the mine's financial contribution over the past several years. The significant portion of the Crow Nation's non-Federal revenues come from the Absaloka Mine. In 2010, these revenues accounted for approximately 40% of the Nation's non-Federal budget. WRI employs a variety of skilled, managerial, professional, and hourly employees, with an annual average salary of over $62,000 and a total annual employment expense of approximately $16 million dollars. The Absaloka Mine is the largest private employer of Crow Tribal members on a reservation that struggles with an unemployment rate that exceeds 47%. More than 70% of the mine's 163 member workforce consists of Crow Tribal members and affiliates. Without question, the Absaloka Mine is critical to the Crow Nation's financial independence now, over the past 37 years, and well into the future.

The Absaloka Mine continues to struggle financially with competition from the larger Powder River coal mines, and with the competitive advantage provided to Powder River coal through the impact of a price differential created by sulfur (SO2) emissions allowances under Title IV of the Clean Air Act. The competitiveness and the continued operation of the mine has been significantly facilitated by the tax benefits made possible by the Indian Coal Production Tax Credits ("the ICPTC") included in the 2005 Energy Policy Act and beginning in 2006. The ICPTCs neutralized the coal price differential related to the SO2 emission allowances. Without the ICPTC, the Absaloka Mine would have ceased to operate, thereby ending a substantial revenue source for the Crow Nation. Continuance of the ICPTC is critical to the future of the Absaloka Mine and the stability of revenue to the Crow Nation.

The Crow Nation is proud of its 37-year partnership with Westmoreland on the Absaloka Mine. The Crow Nation seeks to ensure the continued economic viability of the Absaloka Mine, as the Tribal revenue and jobs that it provides are an overriding imperative for the Nation and its citizens.

B. Many Stars CTL Project

The Crow Nation has been working since 2008 to develop a very significant Coal-to-Liquids (CTL) project within the Crow Indian Reservation called the Many Stars CTL Project. The Project will consist of a new surface coal mine and a proven direct coal liquefaction process plant that sequesters CO_2, uses less water and is more efficient than conventional indirect coal liquefaction projects operating in the world today. This clean-coal technology based project offers the best opportunity for the Crow Nation to monetize our currently stranded, lower-quality coal assets and is a critical economic necessity for the Nation. The CTL project will also provide a critically needed key domestic energy source to the United States and help reduce America's dependence on foreign oil.

However, due to the recent economic downturn and investor concerns about future government policy towards CTL and uncertain permitting requirements to allow carbon sequestration, this project has been struggling to move forward. Even with the currently robust commodity market for transportation fuels, project risk due to historical uncertainties with such commodity markets is still a deterrent to investors.

The Many Stars CTL Project will target conversion of up to 2 billion tons of Crow coal over the life of the project, initially producing 6–8,000 barrels of liquid products per day and ultimately expanding to produce up to 50,000 barrels or more of liquid products per day. The Crow coal would be converted to ultra-clean fuels, such as synthetic jet fuel and diesel fuel at an estimated yield of 1.5 to 2 barrels of liquid product per ton of coal. Thus, when considered in traditional oil and gas terms, this project has the opportunity to responsibly develop and monetize a world-class 3–4 billion barrel oilfield.

For the Crow people, the success of the Many Stars Project is absolutely critical to end decades of poverty and create the long term economic viability of the Crow Nation. The first phase of the integrated surface mine and CTL plant will create up to 2,000 jobs during an initial three year construction period with the expectation that a significant portion of these jobs would continue as the plant is expanded during the subsequent 10–15 years. The number of permanent operations jobs is expected to grow from 250 to 900 upon the commencement of initial operations of both the mine and plant. The jobs created by this project would include high level positions, such as engineers and managers, as well as skilled trades (mechanics, electricians, welders). In addition, income generated by the project could serve to support the Nation's severely underfunded education and health care programs and support the development of key infrastructure on the Crow Reservation to improve the lives of its citizens.

C. Other Crow Coal Development

For many years, members of the Crow Nation have watched a nearly continuous stream of unit trains cross the Reservation every day on the BNSF Railway, carrying someone else's coal to market. The Nation has active plans to develop several billion tons of ultra-low-sulfur coal located in the southeastern portion of the Reservation, for markets that the Absaloka Mine is not well-positioned to serve. These markets could include exports to Asia, which are currently constrained by port terminal capacity on the west coast, as well as difficulty in permitting new coal terminals generally.

D. Oil and gas Development

During 2005–2008, the Crow Nation leased substantial areas of the Reservation for oil and gas exploration and development, using Indian Mineral Development Act agreements. Unfortunately, the independent oil and gas companies who leased these lands did not discover any conventional oil plays like the Bakken formation in northeastern Montana and North Dakota. Instead, the conventional oil exploration work under these agreements resulted in dry holes.

This leasing activity did prove the existence of substantial shallow natural gas reserves on the Crow Reservation. In August, 2009, Ursa Major (an independent oil & gas company from Oklahoma) began delivering the first Tribal natural gas into the interstate pipeline system from the northeastern portion of the Reservation. Further full-field development of Ursa Major's gas field has been slowed by low natural gas prices, coupled with the $6,500 per well APD fee charged by the BLM.

Following the crash in oil prices and the credit markets in late-2008, the industry's interest in leasing Crow oil and gas lands evaporated, and most development plans were suspended. Recently, we have begun to see some renewed interest, as evidenced by drilling plans for this year on a heavy oil prospect in the Pryor area on the western portion of the Reservation, but the $6500 APD fee currently in place reduces the interest of potential developers.

The Nation will continue to pursue oil and gas development, knowing that there are substantial natural gas resources on the Reservation, trusting that the current heavy oil prospect will prove economic, and hoping that our luck will improve on locating other conventional oil resources.

E. Wind Energy

The Crow Reservation encompasses areas with a significant potential for wind energy development. The Crow Nation has, with the assistance of the Division of Energy and Mineral Development through the Department of the Interior, compiled wind data for the past several years, which indicates a steady and reliable Class 5/6 wind resource in several areas of the Reservation. The most significant resource areas are also located in direct proximity to existing transmission lines, and are relatively easily accessible using existing paved highways and secondary roads. The wind resource areas encompass lands held in a variety of ownership patterns, including tribal trust, individual tribal member allotments (many of which are highly fractionated), and non-Indian fee lands.

F. Hydropower

In 1958, the United States condemned over 5500 acres of Crow Reservation lands for building Yellowtail Dam. Yellowtail Dam became operational in 1966. The dam generates over a half billion kilowatt hours of power per year, even during drought conditions. To date, the power generation revenues have exceeded $600 million dollars. Although the Crow Nation did receive a few million dollars for the land taken to create Yellowtail Dam, the Crow Nation has never received any payment from the ongoing revenue from power generation.

The recent Crow Water Rights Settlement Act of 2010 grants the Nation exclusive rights to develop and market hydropower from the Yellowtail Afterbay Dam (immediately downstream from the main Dam). Based on previous Bureau of Reclamation studies, the Yellowtail Afterbay should support the economic development of a small, low-head hydropower facility with an estimated capacity of 10–15 Megawatts. The Nation is currently commissioning a feasibility study to confirm that potential, and to evaluate transmission and marketing opportunities. Our study should be complete in a few months, and provide the necessary information to finance and construct the hydropower facility within the next two years.

The Nation is considering using this hydropower production to supply the local rural cooperatives that provide electric power to the Reservation, to replace their current supplies of low-cost Federal hydropower which will no longer be available in a few years. It also appears that the Afterbay hydropower development could improve water quality in the blue-ribbon trout fishery on the Big Horn River.

IV. Obstacles to Continued Development of Crow Energy

A. Laws and BIA Procedures Impeding Energy Development.

Despite the fact that the Crow Nation has substantial resources, numerous practical problems arise from the previously described history. The Crow Nation and our energy development partners have experienced, and continue to experience, systematic problems in trying to create energy development and the new jobs that would be associated with that development. The Bureau of Indian Affairs ("BIA") consistently creates barriers and delays to resource development.

For example, for an oil and gas lease approved by the Nation in January of 2005, development did not begin until September of 2007 because of an extremely slow BIA approval process. Within the approval process of that lease, an inventory of Tribally-owed net mineral acres was reported as 94,000 acres. However, after the lessee expended large amounts of time and money reexamining mineral title information, an additional 50,000 net Tribal mineral acres was identified and confirmed. An error of this magnitude would be simply unacceptable in many contexts, but in our experience it is not surprising and is far from unique.

BIA records for surface and mineral ownership are often erroneous, missing and out of date. These problems cause significant delay in preparation of environmental documents and overall land records necessary for business transactions. The BIA lacks the necessary staffing to provide accurate information on Reservation surface and mineral ownership, and to resolve additional questions that arise. It is extremely difficult to compete with off-reservation development because of these problems. Many companies view this, in addition to all other problems, as another prohibitive cost of doing business within the Crow Reservation.

Recent BIA procedures have made it increasingly difficult to carry out exploration programs for energy and other minerals on the Reservation. For example, coal exploration involves drilling core holes to verify the quantity and quality of coal, which take only a few days to drill, are accessed by existing undeveloped roads, and are fully reclaimed after completion. The BIA now requires full appraisals approved by the Office of the Special Trustee prior to obtaining consents from the allotted surface owners to drill the core holes and even to cross other allotments to reach the drill sites. These procedures, along with environmental assessments, result in long delays in exploration programs that could otherwise be completed in a matter of months.

The obstacles posed by these procedures are even more prohibitive for other mineral exploration, such as bentonite, which require a large number of auger samples that have even less environmental impact and involve much smaller amounts of recoverable minerals.

Finally, apart from the costs and delays caused by BIA staffing shortages and unnecessary procedures, laws that limit the duration of commercial leases on Tribal lands also impede development of large long-term projects such as the Many Stars CTL project. Many of these obstacles could be addressed by Congressional legislation such as the Indian Energy bill developed last year by the Senate Committee on Indian Affairs and introduced last session.

B. Inability to Plan on Continued Availability of Federal Income Tax Incentives

There are several current federal tax incentives for economic development in Indian Country, including an accelerated depreciation provision, an Indian wage tax credit, and the Indian Coal Production Tax Credit. However, the accelerated depreciation and wage tax credit both have substantial limitations that severely limit their usefulness for major Tribal energy development projects.

More importantly, all of these tax incentives will expire again within the next 2 years, and in the past they have been extended only one year at a time. For major Tribal energy projects, such as a coal mine or a CTL project with 6–10 year development lead times, the inability to rely on the continued availability of these incentives means that they cannot be factored into the economic evaluations that are necessary for investment decisions.

As further explained below, permanent extensions and appropriate modifications to these existing tax incentives would facilitate jobs and economic development, particularly energy development, on the Crow Reservation and for all of Indian Country.

C. The BLM "APD Fee"

Beginning with the FY 2008 Appropriations Act for the Department of the Interior, Congress required the Bureau of Land Management ("BLM") to charge a $4,000 fee to process every Application for Permit to Drill ("APD") on the federal and Indian lands on which it supervises oil and gas development activity. The APD Fee has since been increased by subsequent appropriations legislation to $6,500 for each new well. The Crow Nation has continually protested the application of this fee to tribal lands, and has sought relief in numerous ways, but to date, no solution has been reached.

This $6,500 fee compares to drilling permit fees of less than $100 off the Reservation in the State of Montana. Obviously, it is a disincentive to explore for oil and gas on Indian lands compared to off-reservation State and fee lands. As indicated above, it has been a major factor in the suspension of additional natural gas field exploration and development on the Crow Reservation by our partner, Ursa Major, who also holds leases outside the Reservation. The APD fee is a particular burden for the type of shallow (less than 1500' deep), low-producing gas wells being drilled by Ursa Major. The cost of completing those types of wells is less than $150,000 each, so the APD Fee represents a large portion of the capital investment necessary to bring additional wells into production.

The APD Fee also discourages efficient development and slows exploration efforts. For exploratory "wildcat" drilling where success is not a sure thing, the developer can only afford to get permits for a couple of wells at a time, see if they hit gas, and if so, file APD's for a couple more and repeat the cycle. Without the high APD Fee, the developer would be able to obtain many permits and immediately drill additional wells if the first ones are successful. Considering the lead time for issuance of the drilling permits (60–90 days), the APD Fee causes delays of up to a year developing a handful of new wildcat wells, in addition to adding tens of thousands dollars of non-productive costs that limit the Nation's ability to charge taxes and royalties on the future production.

V. Proposed Solutions

A. Federal Tax Incentive Legislation

1. Indian Coal Production Tax Credit

The 2005 Energy Policy Act provided the Indian Coal Production Tax Credit beginning in tax year 2006, based upon the number of tons of Indian coal produced and sold to an unrelated party. "Indian coal" is coal produced from reserves owned by an Indian Tribe, or held in trust by the United States for the benefit of an Indian Tribe, as of June 14, 2005. The tax credit is calculated by totaling the number of tons of Indian coal produced and sold, then multiplying that number by $1.50 (for calendar years 2006 through 2010). For tax years between 2010 and December 31, 2012, the total number is multiplied by $2.00.

The origin of this production tax credit began with the goal of neutralizing the impact of price differentials created by sulfur (SO_2) emissions allowances, thereby keeping Indian coal competitive in the regional market. Without the credit, the Crow's Absaloka mine would have lost its supply contract and likely been closed in 2005, which would have had a devasting impact on the Nation given that this mine provides a significant portion of the Nation's government's operating budget. The tax credit has worked to keep the mine competitive and open. Now, in 2011, this tax credit remains critically important because, without it, the mine's economic viability would be in serious jeopardy. This tax credit remains critical to the current operation of the existing Absaloka Mine and provides sufficient incentive to help us attract additional investment for future energy projects. In order to protect existing operations and encourage growth, the Indian Coal Production Tax Credit should be made permanent, should be allowed to be used against alternative minimum tax, and the requirement that the coal be sold to an unrelated person should be deleted to allow and encourage facilities owned, in whole or in part, by Indian Nations to participate and benefit from the credit.

2. Accelerated Depreciation Allowance

Included in the *Omnibus Budget Reconciliation Act of 1993*, Pub. L. 103–66, 107 Stat. 558–63, codified at 26 U.S.C. 168(j), 38(b), and 45(A), are two Indian reservation-based Federal tax incentives designed to increase investment and employment on Indian lands. The theory behind these incentives was that they would act in tandem to encourage *private sector* investment and economic activity on Indian lands across the United States. Neither incentive is available for gaming-related infrastructure or activities. The incentives—an accelerated depreciation allowance for "qualified property" placed in service on an Indian reservation and an Indian employment credit to employers that hire "qualified employees"—expired on

December 31, 2003, and have been included in the short-term "extenders packages" of expiring tax incentives since that time.

Energy projects require significant equipment and physical infrastructure, and involve the hiring of large numbers of employees. Crow is not alone in our resource holdings; for several Indian nations, estimates of proven and undeveloped energy resources on Indian lands suggest that revenues to tribal owners would exceed tens of billions in current dollars. As the energy development market improves and the federal programs enacted in the 2005 pro-development energy law, the *Indian Tribal Energy Development and Self Determination Act* (Pub. L. 109–58), energy-related activity on Indian lands will increase substantially in the years ahead.

Unfortunately, one-year or two-year extensions of the accelerated-depreciation provision do not provide an incentive for investment of new capital in Indian country for significant energy projects. Development of major projects generally takes a decade or longer. Investors need certainty that the benefit will be available when the project initiates operations in order to factor that benefit into their projected economic models, as well as investment decisions. A permanent extension would address this problem, making the incentive attractive to investors in long-term energy projects on Indian lands.

As currently written, the depreciation allowance could be interpreted to exclude certain types of energy-related infrastructure related to energy resource production, generation, transportation, transmission, distribution and even carbon sequestration activities. We recommend that language be inserted to statutorily clarify that this type of physical infrastructure expressly qualifies for the accelerated depreciation provision. In proposing this clarification, it is not our objective to eliminate non-energy activities that might benefit from the depreciation allowance. Indeed, if adopted, the language we propose would not discourage other forms of economic development in Indian country.

By providing this clarifying language and this permanent extension, the accelerated depreciation provision will finally accomplish its purpose—enhancing the ability of Indian nations to attract energy industry partners to develop long-term projects utilizing the vast Indian resources available.

3. Indian Employment Wage Credit

The 1993 Act also included an "Indian employment wage credit" with a cap not to exceed 20 percent (20%) of the excess of qualified wages and health insurance costs that an employer pays or incurs. "Qualified employees" are defined as enrolled members of an Indian tribe or the spouse of an enrolled member of an Indian tribe, where substantially all of the services performed during the period of employment are performed within an Indian reservation, and the principal residence of such employee while performing such services is on or near the reservation in which the services are to be performed. *See* 26 U.S.C. 45(c)(1)(A)-(C). The employee will not be treated as a "qualified employee" if the total amount of annual employee compensation exceeds $35,000.

As written, the wage tax credit is completely ineffective and does not attract private-sector investment in energy projects within Indian country. The provision is too complicated and private entities conclude that the cost and effort of calculating the credit outweighs any benefit that it may provide. We therefore propose that the wage and health credit be revised along the lines of the much-heralded Work Opportunity Tax Credit, which is less complicated and more likely to be used by the business community. We propose retaining the prohibition contained in the existing wage and health credit against terminating and rehiring an employee and propose to alter the definition of the term "Indian Reservation" to capture legitimate opportunities for employing tribal members who live on their reservations, even though the actual business activity may be off-reservation. This amendment would allow the Indian Employment Wage Credit to more effectively fulfill the purpose for which it was originally enacted.

B. Eliminate the BLM APD Fee on Indian Lands

The current APD fee of $6500 is a hindrance to the Crow Nation's goal of developing its oil and gas resource. The disparity between the cost for drilling on tribal lands under federal jurisdiction versus lands under state jurisdiction prevents any meaningful economic development of the reserves existing on the Crow Reservation. The federal government should not, through its' trust responsibility, charge administrative fees that prohibit or render economically inefficient, the development of tribal trust assets. Indian lands should be exempted from BLM's APD fee.

C. Need for Government Support for the Many Stars CTL Project

Several CTL projects have been announced in the U.S.; however, all of these projects are struggling due to the high financial commitment needed to plan and implement these projects in an uncertain economic and energy policy environment. Investors and banks are reticent to fund "first of a kind" projects, even though the technology has been proven commercially in other countries and in demonstration plants here in the United States. As a comparison, China is moving forward rapidly in the CTL sector, with 12 sites already producing at commercial demonstration scale of 4–8,000 barrels per day with four commercial projects nearing start of construction at capacities up to 80,000 barrels/day.

Based on the foregoing, the following key actions are crucial for the viability of the Crow's Many Stars CTL Project:

- Grant the Department of Defense and other federal agencies the ability to enter into long-term, guaranteed fixed-price contracts that will underpin the commercial framework needed for these types of long-term CTL projects;
- Extend the expiration date of the current 50-cents per gallon alternative fuel excise tax credit for a definitive time period rather than year-to-year extensions as has been done recently. Since it could take roughly 6–10 years for these types of projects to become fully planned, implemented, and operational, investors are concerned that the incentives will expire before the plant starts up. Consider providing the tax credit for a period of 10 years following start-up for those projects starting construction prior to 2015.
- Support a twenty percent (20%) investment tax credit for each CTL plant placed in service before the same future date, and/or allow 100 percent (100%) expensing of investments in the year of capital outlay for any CTL plant in operation by the same future date.
- Support DOE and DOD alternative fuel development programs as part of a comprehensive energy policy that supports the full spectrum of energy technologies and provides a level playing field for developing new innovation in clean coal technology to meet national environmental goals.
- Remove general uncertainty in energy policy that will provide investors confidence to support new innovation and major investment in the clean coal sector. Our observation is that policy uncertainty with respect to clean coal support equates to paralysis in trying to move the Many Stars CTL Project forward with its investors.

VI. Conclusion

Given our vast mineral resources, the Crow Nation can, and should, be self-sufficient. We seek to develop our mineral resources in an economically sound, environmentally responsible and safe manner that is consistent with Crow culture and beliefs. The Crow people are tired of saying that we are resource rich and cash poor.

We respectfully request your assistance in setting the foundation to make our vision a reality. We have been working to develop our energy resources and to remove obstacles to successful development. We hope to build a near-term future when our own resources, in our own hands, provide for the health, hopes and future of our people.

It is critical that Congress act to protect Indian nations' sovereignty over their natural resources and secure Indian nations as the primary governing entity over their own homelands. This will have numerous benefits for the local communities as well as the federal government. The Crow Nation has been an ally of the United States all through its history.

Today, the Crow Nation desires to develop its vast natural resources not only for itself, but to once again help the United States with a new goal—achieving energy independence, securing a domestic supply of valuable energy, and reducing its dependence on foreign oil. Many members of the Crow Nation are veterans of the United States Armed Forces and we have a special understanding and respect for what it could mean to our sons and daughters in coming years if all of our energy needs were met here at home.

It is time for the Crow Nation to become an energy partner. However, our vision can only become a reality with your assistance. I strongly feel that the vision starts today. Mr. Chairman and Committee members, thank you again for the opportunity to testify on Indian Energy before you today. I would be happy to answer any questions.

————

Mr. YOUNG. Thank you for your testimony, and what we will do is go through the panel, and then we will ask questions, and I hope that everyone is listening very intently. Mr. Tex Hall, Chairman of the Three Affiliated Tribes of the Fort Berthold Reservation. Tex, you are up.

STATEMENT OF MR. TEX HALL, CHAIRMAN, THREE AFFILIATED TRIBES OF THE FORT BERTHOLD RESERVATION

Mr. HALL. Chairman Young, and Members of the Committee, my name is Ihbudah Hishi, Red Tipped Arrow, but for today, it is Tex Hall, my English name. It is a great honor to present on behalf of my Tribal Nation, Mandan, Hidatsa and Arikara, on the Fort Berthold, West Central, North Dakota.

I join my colleague, Scott Russell, in congratulating the Subcommittee on Indian and Alaska Native Affairs, and I appreciate this Subcommittee for having this hearing to evaluate energy development opportunities, and that is what we are talking about today—huge opportunities.

And our reservation is located in the largest oil play in the United States. It is the Bakken Formation. The USGS, the United States Geological Survey, has estimated 4.3 billion recoverable barrels of oil.

Mr. Chairman, like you said, they estimated 7 billion out of Prudhoe Bay and have recovered 17 billion. However, unfortunately, oil and gas exploration has lagged behind energy development on our reservation, as compared to the State of North Dakota, largely because of unnecessary red tape and bureaucratic delays at the Interior Department, and the EPA, in processing the necessary approvals under Federal law.

As you know, oil and gas exploration is subject to extensive Federal oversight and overview. Leasing, permitting, royalty collection, royalty payments, involve five separate agencies; BIA, Bureau of Indian Affairs; BLM, Bureau of Land Management; MMS, now Bureau of Ocean Energy Management; the Office of Special Trustee for American Indians; and the Environmental Protection Agency.

In order to comply with the many Federal laws and regulations that apply to Indian mineral activities, the Interior Department has developed a 49 step process for obtaining Federal approvals.

This 49 step process can take as long as two years to complete to get the permit to drill. In contrast, with our State of North Dakota, the process for approving oil and gas exploration activities on non-Indian lands involves four steps.

Oil and gas leases in North Dakota don't need governmental approval, and it only takes about a week-and-a-half to process an application for a permit to drill, and that is just unfair.

I believe that we have to find a way to streamline this process for Federal review, and approval of individual Indian and Tribal leases, and make it less complicated, more efficient, and at the same time, however, it must be done to ensure that the Federal Government will continue to fulfill its trust responsibility to our Tribal Nation.

This can be accomplished by placing all Federal authority in one agency on our reservation, such as through the one stop shop that we were working through with the Bureau of Indian Affairs and in the Senate.

However, there must be adequate funding to make sure that all of those five agencies come on to the reservation so that the approvals are done on the reservation, and not done through our Region 8 office in Denver.

I can't imagine trying to approve a permit from Denver, which is three or four States away from our tribal lands. I have been working for the past three-and-a-half years to overcome these Interior regulatory obstacles that we are facing so our Indian mineral owners on the Fort Berthold Reservation can have the same opportunities for energy exploration that exists on State or private lands outside the reservation.

We have approximately 8,000 allottees on my reservation, and they are patiently waiting for development and for their opportunity for oil and gas wells to occur.

As far as mitigating the impacts of oil and gas development a substantial part of revenue from oil and gas production of our land comes from taxes, revenues that our tribal government needs to take, but has a massive toll on the roads, and so it is a blessing, and it is a curse when oil and gas are developed, or is found on your reservation.

So we are frantically trying to secure enough funding to make sure that there are no stranded wells because there is no adequate road system. So these revenues for our tribal roads are sorely needed.

And, Mr. Chairman, I am running out of time, and so I have a copy of our latest version of our recommendation papers, and are attached to my statement, and I ask that it be made part of the record for today's hearing.

[The prepared statement of Mr. Hall follows:]

Statement of Tex G. Hall, Chairman,
Mandan, Hidatsa and Arikara Nation of the Fort Berthold Reservation

Good morning, Chairman Young, Ranking Member Boren, and other members of the Subcommittee on Indian and Alaska Native Affairs. My name is Tex Hall, or Ihbudah Hishi, which means "Red Tipped Arrow." I am honored to present this testimony as the Chairman of the Mandan, Hidatsa and Arikara Nation of the Fort Berthold Reservation in North Dakota (MHA Nation).

Let me start my testimony by expressing my appreciation to the Subcommittee for having this hearing to evaluate energy development opportunities on Indian lands.

Fort Berthold Oil and Gas Regulatory Issues

The Fort Berthold Reservation is located in the heart of the Bakken Formation, which is the largest continuous oil accumulation within the lower 48 states. In 2008, the U.S. Geological Survey (USGS) estimated that the Formation contains between 3 billion and 4.3 billion barrels of recoverable oil. This USGS assessment compares favorably to the agency's most recent assessment of oil contained within the Arctic National Wildlife Refuge (ANWR). As of 2005, the USGS assessment for ANWR was that it contained between 4.3 billion and 11.8 billion barrels of recoverable oil.

Unfortunately, oil and gas exploration on the Fort Berthold Reservation has been lagging behind energy development on non-Indian lands in North Dakota, largely because of unnecessary red tape and bureaucratic delays at the Interior Department, in processing the necessary approvals under Federal law.

As you know, oil and gas exploration is subject to extensive Federal oversight and review. Leasing, permitting, royalty collection, and royalty payment activities involve five separate agencies: the Bureau of Indian Affairs, the Bureau of Land Management, the Bureau of Ocean Energy Management, the Office of the Special Trustee for American Indians and the Environmental Protection Agency. In order to comply with the many Federal laws and regulations that apply to Indian mineral activities, the Interior Department has developed a 49-step process for obtaining Federal approvals involving oil and gas exploration. This 49-step process can take as long as two (2) years to complete.

In contrast, the process for approving oil and gas exploration activities on non-Indian lands in North Dakota involves just 4 steps. Oil and gas leases don't need governmental approval and, according to the North Dakota Industrial Commission, it only takes about a week and a half to process an application for a permit to drill.

I believe that we must find a way to streamline the process for federal review and approval of individual Indian and tribal mineral leases and agreements and make it less complicated and more efficient. At the same time, however, it must be done in a way that ensures the federal government will continue to fulfill its trust responsibility to the MHA Nation. This can be accomplished by placing all federal authority in one agency on our Reservation, such as through a One Stop Shop Office, as discussed in more detail below. There must be adequate funding that ensures the federal officials responsible for approving and regulating these leases and agreements on the ground are adequately qualified and that there is sufficient agency staff to meet the demand that comes with this extensive oil boom in the Bakken Formation.

I have been working for the past 3 ½ years to overcome the Interior regulatory obstacles we are facing, so that Indian mineral owners on the Fort Berthold Reservation can have the same opportunities for energy exploration that exist on private lands outside of the Reservation. Prior to my recent election as Chairman, and since our Reservation has more than 8,000 allottee owners, I formed the Fort Berthold Land and Mineral Owners Association several years ago, to represent individual allottee owners on oil and gas regulatory issues.

As the Chairman of the MHA Nation, I now have the responsibility for our tribal lands as well as our individual Indian lands. Our focus must be on maximizing the economic benefit that the MHA Nation and its members can receive from the oil and gas resources under our lands. At the same time, our lands must be protected by appropriate federal and tribal regulations, adopted and enforced on a cooperative basis, which protects our environment and our people.

Mitigating the Impacts of Oil and Gas Development

A substantial amount of revenue from oil and gas production on our land comes from taxes, revenues that the our tribal government needs to help mitigate the massive toll on our roads, law enforcement, fire and emergency protection, and environment that comes with this oil boom. Oil and gas is a nonrenewable resource. Once it is extracted and sold by the oil companies that lease our lands, it is gone forever. As a result of the continued threat of double State and tribal taxation on Indian energy development on the Reservation, the tax revenue that the MHA Nation receives from production on tribal lands has not been maximized. Indian tribes should be the primary beneficiaries of the tax revenue that is generated from energy production on Indian land. These revenues are sorely needed to keep up with the overwhelming burden that oil and gas production puts on our roads, our natural and human resources.

While the oil and gas industry has brought increased economic opportunities to the MHA Nation, those increased opportunities have not come without costs. The three most visible of those costs are the virtual destruction of many of our Reservation roads, the advent of new law enforcement and public safety needs, and the negative environmental impacts associated with oil and gas development.

1. Reservation Roads Costs. Let me start with the impact on our roads. The Fort Berthold Reservation encompasses approximately 1 million acres, approximately 1,544 square miles, and 1,520 miles of roads, a sizable percentage of which are used by the oil and gas industry. The Reservation encompasses parts of six North Dakota Counties: Mountrail, McKenzie, Ward, McLean, Dunn and Mercer. Approximately half of the Reservation consists of tribal and allotted trust land. Of the 1,520 miles of roads, more than 70%, or 1,200 miles, are in the Bureau of Indian Affairs (BIA) inventory system. Roads in the BIA inventory are broken down as follows:

- Rural minor arterial roads: 141.2 miles
- Community streets: 28.7 miles
- Rural major collector roads: 191.5 miles
- Rural local roads: 729.5 miles
- City minor arterial streets: 6.8 miles

In addition to the 1,200 miles of BIA/Tribal Indian Reservation roads described above, there are also approximately 664.4 miles of county roads and 150 miles of state highways within the Reservation. There also is an undetermined amount of private roads and abandoned BIA roads that are impacted to various extents by the oil and gas industry. Unfortunately, this ownership pattern has made it difficult, and in some cases, impossible, to keep these roads maintained in a manner which is safe for both the industry and tribal members.

The current road system was not constructed to withstand the weight and volume of heavy truck traffic that accompanies the oil boom. The damage being done daily is enormous, and the MHA Nation does not nearly have the resources to keep up with the burden. For example, the MHA Nation recently had to break up the existing pavement and resurface it with additional gravel paid for by the Nation. The estimated cost was over $500,000. The work was necessary because the oil traffic literally destroyed the road faster than any paving contract could repair it.

Despite the safety hazards presented, the Nation was forced to pay for this work itself, because the BIA's roads maintenance funding distribution formula is based almost exclusively on maintaining roads utilized by normal non-industrial traffic. At a minimum this year, 56.2 miles of BIA/Tribal roads need to be reconstructed immediately, with more reconstruction becoming necessary in the future. According to the BIA Roads Engineer, the estimated cost for adequate design and reconstruction of the inferior roads is approximately $1.5 million per mile, which equals over $84.3 million.

The current roads on the Reservation are also beyond their life span. The highways were built with 2 inches of bituminous asphalt in the 1970s-80s, not enough to withstand the heavy traffic that comes with oil trucks and oil-related traffic. The MHA Nation has currently over 2,500 trucks working on the Reservation; and each oil well from drilling to production takes over 2,024 trips per year per truck. The MHA Nation is anticipating over 200 new oil wells this coming year, which will triple the number of trucks on our roads.

According to our tribal records 57.7% of the Reservation roads are gravel, 26.6% are paved and 16% are primitive dirt. Much of the current system remains inaccessible to drilling and is in need of immediate upgrade to allow access to well sites; we cannot afford to have potential stranded wells. In addition to the immediate repairs and upgrades needed, we estimate that it will cost millions of dollars per year to maintain the Reservation roads as long as the oil boom lasts. The current BIA budget to maintain our road system is a paltry $456,000.

Travel is hazardous even in good weather. The damage which has been and will continue to be inflicted on the tribal, county, and state road system has made travel on those roads very hazardous. As a result, our traffic accidents and fatalities have dramatically increased since 2007 when the oil activity began. Presently, there are so many potholes and ruts on our tribal roads that the MHA Nation simply cannot keep up with them. In fact, many of our roads are so deteriorated, that when we can find the money to repair a small stretch, the patch does not hold and the next section of road just falls away. This winter's snow accumulation has doubled our snow removal budget and our small crew has to work around the clock to keep our roads open for this oil traffic. For all of these reasons, our roads currently present a very real danger to our school busses, emergency vehicles, the general public, and even the vehicles operated by the oil and gas industry itself. Those roads are also costing our citizens, our governments and the oil and gas industry itself thousands of dollars a year in vehicle repairs and replacements, and this situation is and will continue to stifle economic growth.

Let me make it clear that the MHA Nation is already doing its part. We are currently supplementing the BIA roads budget with over $2 million in tribal funds. We are so concerned with the safety of the public and of the oil and gas workers themselves that we are spending as much of our own money as possible to address this problem. Unfortunately, that is simply not enough. Thus, we need your help in the form of a practical and equitable adjustment of the allocation of oil and gas related tax dollars. The MHA Nation is not looking for a windfall; it is simply looking for the funds necessary to allow this economic boom to continue in a safe and responsible manner.

Mr. Chairman, nothing is more important to any of us than the safety of our citizens and to put it bluntly—on these roads, our citizens are not safe.

2. Law Enforcement Costs. In addition, the MHA Nation has very serious and very pressing law enforcement and public safety problems that have to be addressed immediately, and those problems can only be addressed with increased dollars. The influx of new oil and gas workers has created a great deal of strain on our already severely underfunded tribal law enforcement and highway law enforcement systems. At present, the MHA Nation can only afford to employ thirteen (13) law enforcement officers—and this is after the Nation supplements the federal law enforcement dollars that we receive by approximately $1 million a year.

These thirteen officers are, according to testimony presented to the Congress by the Bureau of Indian Affairs in 2010, only 1/3 of the minimum number of officers that we require just to service our own Reservation population of approximately 12,500 (approximately 10,000 of whom are Indian). This does not include the thousands who are on the Reservation on a temporary basis just to work. Add to this the number of officers that we now require in order to serve the increasing population from new oil and gas workers in our communities, the increased traffic, the large land base our officers must cover, the increased number of automobile accidents and increased fatalities created by our ever deteriorating roads and the heavy traffic, and you can begin to see just how serious our situation really is.

The substantial increase in population brought on by oil boom on the Reservation has brought with it an increased burden on law enforcement. A recent article in the Bismarck Tribune reported that police calls in Williston, a city just west of our Reservation and also in the Bakken formation, have increased 250% in the last year. We face the same problem on our Reservation because of the distances our officers have to travel, and the substantial increase in calls for police assistance. Our police response time has now risen to up to 1 hour in some cases, which is unacceptable. This coupled with the significantly increased costs of repairing police vehicles which are traveling 1,500 miles or more a day on our deteriorated roads, has left our small tribal police department and its budget stretched to the breaking point. For all of these reasons, we need more law enforcement resources in order to protect the public and without those resources, people will continue to suffer unnecessarily.

The MHA Nation is in the process of constructing a health clinic. The clinic is underfunded and my Administration has made it a priority to find sufficient funds from all available sources to build a larger and better facility and one that has an emergency response capability for our Nation members and for oil and gas potential accidents. In addition, we need ambulance and air ambulatory services that will deliver much needed critical care. Additional funding is needed to build houses to recruit and support doctors, nurses and clinic staff.

3. Environmental Costs. No one disputes the overwhelming effect that the oil and gas boom in western North Dakota is having on our tribal, county, and local governments, as well as our citizens in western North Dakota. The impact on our roads, infrastructure, law enforcement, emergency services, and particularly our natural environment, has far exceeded the resources our respective governments have to keep up with the burden.

The need for a fair, cooperative and comprehensive oil and gas tax and regulatory system on the Fort Berthold Reservation is critical as we move forward to deal with the continuing onslaught that comes with this economic boom. Mr. Chairman and members of the Subcommittee, it is particularly important to recognize that we all have a responsibility to ensure that the oil and gas industry is held accountable for the responsible development of our resources. This is particularly true when it comes to the dust, the fumes, and the damage to our roads, our horses and cattle, and the increased danger to our people as a result of the heavy truck traffic that comes with oil and gas activity. We must all be concerned about the transportation and use of the chemicals used in the oil fields of western North Dakota and to make sure that it is done in a safe and responsible manner.

The MHA Nation needs more revenue to catch up to and get ahead of the enormous burden the oil and gas development is putting on our roads and infrastructure, our law enforcement and emergency response personnel, and to help put an effective regulatory and inspection system in place to protect our natural and human resources. This must come from all available federal funding sources, as well as Congressional support of an amendment to existing Indian energy legislation that levels the playing field on energy tax issues by clarifying that Indian tribes have the exclusive authority to tax energy development on Indian lands.

Outstanding Regulatory Issues

We must have a coordinated regulatory system in place to protect our land and our resources while we promote responsible development. Over the past several years, our Allottee Association has developed very detailed recommendations for addressing the outstanding oil and gas regulatory issues on the Reservation. A copy of the latest version of our recommendations paper is attached to my statement.

While we have certainly made progress, there are still many issues which have not been addressed by the Department. Let me highlight for you the most significant of these outstanding issues:

1. Improved Staffing. The Interior Department was not prepared for the level of oil and gas approval requests at Fort Berthold, when leasing and exploration activities began in earnest in 2007. With help from the North Dakota Congressional delegation, we were able to increase staffing for these regulatory activities at both the Fort Berthold Agency and the Great Plains Regional Office. The Department also accepted our recommendation that a "One Stop Shop Office" begin operation at Fort Berthold, in order to ensure that all four Interior agencies are represented in one location and can operate in a coordinated fashion. Unfortunately, Congress has yet to provide funding for the personnel necessary to staff this One Stop Shop Office. As a result, mistakes have been made and leases have been approved at less than market value.

Let me give you one example. In early 2008, the BIA approved a tribal lease executed pursuant to the Indian Mineral Development Act that tied up nearly 42,000 acres. The bonus paid for this lease was $50 per acre, at a time when bonuses for oil and gas leases in the Bakken, including leases on the Reservation, were going for $1000 or more an acre. This is inexcusable.

Last year's energy bill that contained language for funding the One Stop Shop Office did not make it through Congress. Therefore, there is no budget available to continue this concept. The BIA staff still support the need for this important concept and agree the funds should be provided to implement it. I share this view, and urge the Congress to fund and support the concept of a One Stop Shop Office, to streamline the process for the approval of and regulation of Indian oil and gas leases.

It is my understanding that the Obama Administration has requested an additional $1 million in funding for energy development on our Reservation in Fiscal Year 2012, including a $500,000 increase for staff support at the One Stop Shop Office. While this is a step in the right direction and worthy of support, I want to make sure that we are taking a comprehensive approach to the Fort Berthold staffing problems and are not just increasing Interior budgetary authority.

2. Better Communications. The Department of the Interior has now detailed an employee from the Division of Energy and Mineral Development in Lakewood, Colorado to assist the BIA at the Fort Berthold Agency in New Town. This is a positive step. However, more resources are needed. In particular, the Department needs to improve the manner in which it interacts with the 8,000 allottee mineral owners on the Reservation. We have suggested that the Department create an allottee liaison function at the Fort Berthold Agency and also at the Great Plains Regional Office. People appointed as allottee liaisons would serve as the primary point of contact for individual mineral owners who have questions and need specific information about regulatory approvals.

Allottee owners also should be consulted by the Department on issues and specific approvals that affect their mineral interests.

As an additional step to improve communication and transparency, each of the four Interior agencies should issue a monthly report to interested parties on the status of approvals. Each Interior agency also should maintain a periodic in-person presence at the One Stop Shop Office, in order to answer questions from interested parties and to address outstanding regulatory issues.

3. Streamlined Regulatory Procedures. Over the past three years, we have identified a number of areas where the Department can streamline and improve its regulatory procedures. For example, the Interior agencies responsible for various oil and gas leasing activities will each apply a different lease number to the same parcel of allotted or tribal land on the Reservation. My understanding is that these Interior agencies all have different computer systems, with no standardization (or coordination) among these agencies on the assignment of a lease number. In my view, it makes no sense to have three different lease numbers for the same parcel of land under lease. It is confusing to everyone and it slows down the process to have this lack of standardization within the Department on such a critical issue.

A second example of a lack of inter-agency coordination at Interior involves well completion reports. Energy companies have to notify the Department when a well is producing. For some reason, there is a lack of coordination between the Interior agency responsible for the well being drilled (the Bureau of Land Management) and the agency responsible for the royalty payments after the well begins producing (the Bureau of Ocean Energy Management, formerly the Minerals Management Service).

A third problem is the fact that there is significant duplication among the different Interior agencies regarding rental payments being paid on each parcel of leased land. Confusion exists about how these rental payments are to be made once a well moves from being drilled to one that is producing.

All of these coordination problems make it very complicated for an Indian mineral owner (or an energy company) to know what is going on. Royalty checks show up without any identification regarding which parcel is producing oil and natural gas. Approvals involving the Bureau of Land Management have a different lease number for a parcel than the number used by the Bureau of Indian Affairs in originally approving the lease for that same parcel. And there is no auditing process for an Indian mineral owner to verify that any of the payments being received are for the correct amounts. Remarkably, an Indian mineral owner receives a series of individual checks in the mail for each leased parcel, with no information about the purpose of each check or the calculations behind the amounts being disbursed.

4. Better Interior Recordkeeping. The Department needs to modernize its internal recordkeeping processes. The first problem involves the Land Title and Records Office at the Great Plains Regional Office. Numerous title mistakes are still being made by this Office, including life estate ownership, probate, and accounting errors.

And the problem is only going to get worse, as oil exploration activities increase on the Reservation. We need an improved land title verification system and one that can function in the same manner and with the same electronic capabilities as a County land records office in North Dakota.

Second, the Department needs to upgrade its filing and tracking system at Fort Berthold for leases, applications, and other approval requests. There have been far too many situations in which Department officials can't locate paperwork or figure out the status of a pending approval request.

5. New Pipeline Infrastructure. The Fort Berthold Reservation has very little infrastructure to transport oil and natural gas through and outside the Reservation, from the many wells that are now operating on our lands. Since we have almost no pipeline capacity at Fort Berthold, energy companies are primarily using trucks to transport oil from the wells to market. Natural gas can only be transported through a pipeline and so most of it is lost into the atmosphere instead of being gathered and transported to market.

Our lack of pipeline infrastructure is resulting in a significant loss of revenue, taxes, and royalty payments for everyone involved.

We need a comprehensive infrastructure solution that will serve all the Indian mineral owners on the Reservation, in gathering and transporting oil and gas from individual wells. The Department needs to partner with us to ensure that pipeline infrastructure is build on the Reservation as quickly as possible and that it offers a comprehensive solution to our needs in this area, both to ensure public safety and to maximize the use of our energy resources.

6. More Coordination with the State. In 2008, the now former Chairman of the MHA Nation signed a Regulatory Agreement with the State of North Dakota, to improve the coordination between our Nation and the State on certain oil and gas issues. This Agreement is important in that it provides certainty for energy operators on what the rules are and which governmental entity has responsibility for each oil and gas exploration function.

Unfortunately, the State insisted on several provisions that are inconsistent with our Tribe's sovereignty and also inconsistent with Federal standards. As a result, the Agreement has not been approved by the Department and has not been renegotiated. It is sitting on someone's desk at Main Interior, despite being signed almost 3 years ago.

This Regulatory Agreement needs to be renegotiated and approved by all the parties: the Three Affiliated Tribes, the State, and the Department. We should not have to wait so long for the Department to evaluate this Agreement and work with us to fix the problems regarding our sovereignty and how best to meet Federal standards.

7. Improved Interior Decision-making Processes. To improve coordination among the four Interior agencies responsible for different oil and gas regulatory functions, the Department should develop a written Memorandum of Understanding among the affected Interior agencies, outlining the specific authorities and responsibilities of the One Stop Shop Office at Fort Berthold. The purpose of this Memorandum of Understanding should be to create an internal process to resolve issues among Interior agencies and improve the coordination of responsibilities involving oil and gas approvals on the Reservation.

A second step that the Department should consider is the formation of a Fort Berthold Oil and Gas Advisory Committee, to provide the Department with the views of a broad spectrum of stakeholders involved with oil and gas exploration activities. You can see that we have a long list of outstanding regulatory issues at Fort Berthold and we need some type of forum or process to discuss and evaluate these unresolved issues. As energy exploration activities continue to increase rapidly, the pressures on the Interior regulatory system are only going to become worse. Everyone involved in oil and gas activities at Fort Berthold needs an efficient and effective process to develop solutions to our regulatory problems.

8. Communitization Agreements. A further issue involves Communitization Agreements. Indian mineral owners are not being paid their royalties at the same time as non-Indian mineral owners. To remedy this problem, the Bureau of Land Management should require energy companies to apply for a Communitization Agreement at the same time they file an Application for Permit to Drill (APD).

9. EPA Minor Source Rule. My final point involves the proposal by the Environmental Protection Agency (EPA) to promulgate its minor source rule. The MHA Nation is concerned about the impact this new rule may have on oil and gas exploration and has urged the EPA to engage in government-to-government consultations regarding the implementation of this rule before it is finalized.

The Bakken Formation presents a very important opportunity to help improve the energy security of the United States by reducing our dependence on foreign—and volatile—sources for oil and natural gas. The Bakken Formation also can provide numerous benefits to the MHA Nation and its members. Exploration of this important resource is a true "win-win" proposition, as it will help our country increase its domestic energy supplies and it will provide needed financial resources to the MHA Nation and to the more than 8,000 allottee owners on our Reservation.

A Petroleum Refinery on the Fort Berthold Reservation

The MHA Nation has been working for the past eight (8) years to finalize the process under the National Environmental Policy Act (NEPA) to begin construction of its MHA Nation Clean Fuels Refinery Project (Project). Since publication of the Final Environmental Impact Statement (FEIS), the Environmental Protection Agency (EPA) has delayed issuance of a Record of Decision (ROD) for fear of litigation. This litigation fear stems from a few comments that EPA received during the project's comment period which pointed out the absence of an EPA air permit for the Project. Although EPA concluded that the Project qualifies as a minor source which is currently not subject to air permitting requirements under the Clean Air Act (CAA), a handful of comments threatened suit against the EPA and called for further review of the Project. These concerns have halted EPA's efforts to move forward with its issuance of the ROD.

Initially, feedstock for the Project was expected to consist of 10,000 barrels per stream day (BPSD) of synthetic crude oil via existing pipeline from Albert, Canada; 3,000 BPSD of field butane from local suppliers; 6 million standard cubic feet per day of natural gas via existing pipeline; and 300 barrels of bio-diesel or 8,500 bushels per day of soybeans. However, since that time, advances in technology and development of the hydraulic fracturing process have created an abundant supply of Bakken crude produced on and near the Fort Berthold Reservation. Given the cost savings, the Tribe determined that it would be more feasible, and in its best interest, to change the feedstock for the Project from synthetic Canadian crude to Bakken crude. We notified EPA of our decision in December of 2009. Unfortunately, this change raised further EPA questions regarding the air quality and emissions which would result from this change and the overall impact that the change would have on the air quality impact report.

From December 2009 to the present, the EPA withdrew its Prevention of Significant Deterioration (PSD) non-determination letter dated April 2005 and requested additional information from the Nation and its consultants regarding the air quality studies conducted for the Project. The Nation has worked diligently to respond to EPA's concerns, but as of yet, to little or no avail. Although the Nation has conducted an assay of the change in feedstock which clearly demonstrates that the emissions for Bakken are much lower and at times even better than synthetic Canadian crude, EPA is asserting that a complete supplement to the Final EIS may be necessary. This would delay the issuance of a ROD for an additional two (2) years. As a result of all of this EPA-created delay, the Tribe is now finding that it is likely going to face new and additional regulatory requirements before a ROD can be issued.

On March 9, 2011, the Nation met with representatives of the EPA—Region 8 Office, and was advised that issuance of a ROD would not be likely prior to implementation of the EPA's new greenhouse gas regulations which are scheduled to go into effect on July 1, 2011. The basis for the EPA's position is its continued fear of litigation for failing to comply with NEPA. As a result, the EPA—Region 8 Office proffered the following options for the Nation:

- Issue a ROD despite the change in feedstock and supplement the record;
- Supplement the final EIS which will require an additional two (2) years of review;
- Designate the Project as a minor source—which still requires more information; or
- Await implementation of the minor NSR rule for Indian Country to determine whether the Project can be classified as a minor source and therefore, subject to obtaining a minor source permit under the minor NSR rule.

The MHA Nation clearly expressed its support for issuing a ROD and supplementing the record so that it can begin construction of the Project and avoid application of the new EPA greenhouse gas regulations. However, the Region 8 Office indicated that it must defer to the EPA leaders in Washington, D.C., to make the final decision as to whether a ROD may be issued by supplementing the record.

Given all that we have gone through, we are now calling upon Congress to take charge over this matter by providing us with an exception to the greenhouse gas regulations scheduled to go into effect on July 1, 2011, and any other regulations that will likely subject the Project to further delay. We have worked long and hard to meet all of EPA's demands and we feel strongly that we should not have to go through a whole series of new steps simply because EPA has delayed its approvals and decided to change its regulations.

Wind Energy Opportunities in the Great Plains

Mr. Chairman, let me quickly present one final issue: wind energy. As you know, the MHA Nation and the other Tribes in the Great Plains have great wind potential. Unfortunately, many of us are simply too far from the grid to make such development cost effective. To address this problem, we need additional transmission lines and upgraded systems to allow the wind energy that we hope to develop to be moved to the areas where it is needed.

To insure our successful wind energy development, many of the Tribes in the Great Plains have joined together as members of the Intertribal Council On Utility Policy (COUP) Wind Project. This group is currently working with the Western Area Power Administration (WAPA), and views WAPA as its primary market. Today, WAPA is still purchasing coal fired power to meet its hydropower contracts. This does not make good environmental sense, as we have huge amounts of carbon-free wind blowing in our area every day.

In 2009, a Wind and Hydropower Feasibility Study (WHFS) was completed which found that tribal wind projects are feasible, but the study had several shortcomings. First, it failed to show how tribal wind energy will fit into the current purchase and transition systems, given the current contracts that groups like WAPA already have with other energy producers. Second, it did not adequately address new and better ways to integrate wind and hydropower generation in our area. Finally, it did not look carefully enough at ways to increase transmission capacity through the development and construction of a new and more efficient grid. Our Intertribal COUP Project has a team of wind energy and interconnection experts who are ready to complete this study. This additional research is already authorized. We simply need a $1 million appropriation to complete the work this year.

I would also ask the Subcommittee to consider authorizing a 1000 mega watt Intertribal Wind Energy Demonstration Project in our area. The demonstration project that I am proposing would produce clean energy at market rates under long-term, rate-based, fixed price contracts. We believe that such a demonstration project will show that new well planned tribal wind energy systems can produce savings by minimizing or even eliminating the need for supplemental purchases from hydropower producers. If funded, this demonstration project will provide clear energy to WAPA customers, and allow an increased portion of the federal grid system to be used to meet the new clean energy standards that Americans are now demanding.

Conclusion

Chairman Young and members of the Subcommittee, thank you again for the opportunity to highlight for you some of the more significant regulatory issues we face at Fort Berthold and the wind energy opportunities that are before us.

At the appropriate time, I am happy to answer any questions you may have.

———

Mr. YOUNG. That will be done, and I thank you, Tex, and we are going to hear the last witness, and if anybody wants to leave, we do have a series of five votes, and when that last witness is over, you guys can relax, go to the restroom, or do whatever you want to do.

We will be back, I would say, in about 35 minutes, or maybe 40 minutes. So, Mr. Shelly, you are up.

STATEMENT OF BEN SHELLY, PRESIDENT, NAVAJO NATION

Mr. SHELLY. Thank you very much, and good morning, Chairman Young, Committee Members, and also Tribal Leaders. I am Ben Shelly, the President of the Navajo Nation. I want to thank Congressman Luján, and also Congressman Gosar, for their service to the Navajo Nation.

I look forward to working with this Congress, and also President Obama's Administration, in developing a comprehensive tribal energy policy, a policy that promotes the interests of the tribe first.

The relationship between the Navajo Nation and the United States is a complex one, based upon a government-to-government relationship. Nevertheless, this relationship has been less than desirable at times.

It is estimated that 32 percent of the Navajo homes lack electricity; 86 percent, natural gas; 40 percent of Navajo are unemployed; and 40 percent of Navajo live below the Federal poverty line.

As the Navajo Nation President, I take on this as my responsibility. We are all in this together, and we have to work together to create jobs and improve our economy. The key to our prosperity and self-determination is our people and our land.

We hold significant renewable and non-renewable natural resources, including coal, oil, and natural gas. The Navajo Nation is resource rich, and we want development of our resource.

Nevertheless, we have been held back for many reasons. I believe the United States leadership when they tell me that they want to help us develop our resources, but that message seems to get lost with the Federal Government.

I feel that there is too much red tape on our projects. We need a balanced approach that provides for the much-needed development of our lands, while at the same time providing sufficient safeguards.

At the Navajo Nation, we prefer a multi-prong approach to our energy reserve. We are balancing our economic opportunity with our environmental concern. We are taking a realistic view at the following energy package, number one, renewable energy.

And, number two, a viable future with coal, clean coal technology, and a phased approach to emission reduction, and three, alternative energy sources. Desert Rock utilized modern coal technology. The Desert Rock project is a clean coal generating power plant, proposed by the Sithe Corporation in partnership with the Navajo Nation.

Desert Rock will be one of the newest and cleanest coal generating plants in the country. Desert Rock will provide one-third of the Navajo Nation's entire annual budget and allow us to head toward the path of self-determination.

The United States issued a permit in 2008, but rescinded the permit in 2009. Currently, the permit is under appeal by the Navajo Nation. There are many important considerations that a Federal agency must review when proposing rulemaking that will affect the energy development goals of the Navajo Nation.

We are planning to operate our power plant at significant emission reduction. Last, I want to affirm that the Navajo Nation's position concerning uranium mining. Let me be clear that the Navajo Nation opposes uranium mining on our land.

At the same time, the Navajo Nation opposes any budget cuts to the Surface Mining Control and Reclamation Act. That funds the Navajo Nation's AML, programs to clean up over 1,000 scattered, abandoned, and dangerous mines.

From the heart, I would like to say this. We have honored the codetalker. Out of the original 29, we only have one left. We honor them, and most of the people that left the codetalker did not have running water or electric.

Please, honor them, by advancing and helping us with the red tape that we go through with our energy. Recognize us. I want to form an energy team, and a Native energy team will be good for the United States, and for our partners, also with the States and the Federal Government.

If we have employment, we will have taxes, and I think that some of these deficits that we have, that State and Federal governments are going through, will help. We would like to help in that area. Thank you very much.

[The prepared statement of Mr. Shelly follows:]

Statement of Ben Shelly, President, The Navajo Nation

NAVAJO NATION BACKGROUND

The Navajo Nation (Nation) wants to attract businesses and lay down a track for investments in infrastructure, development and renewable energy that will create a stronger-driven, prosperous Nation. We have significant renewable and non-renewable natural resources, including substantial reserves of coal, oil and natural gas.

It has been exciting to be part of a new beginning for our Nation to restructure and streamline, using our fresh ideas and traditional teachings to complete our challenges and lay a solid foundation for future generations.

Our Nation has approximately 300,000 members and covers more than 27,000 square miles within the exterior boundaries of Arizona, New Mexico, and Utah, also occupying parts of 13 counties in those states.

The Navajo people also combat extreme poverty placing the reservation among the lowest echelons of socio-economic indicators for any graphic region in the United States. The latest statistics indicate that 48% of the Navajo people are unemployed and 40% live below the federal poverty line.

Our living conditions are considered substandard. An estimated 25% of homes on the reservation are traditional Navajo dwellings, called hogans. The remaining 75% of housing is comprised of mobile homes, modular buildings, and standard homes. Basic amenities are lacking in the following areas: 31% do not have complete plumbing, 28% do not have operational kitchen facilities, 38% do not have water services, 32% are without electricity, 86% do not have natural gas services, and 60% of the homes lack telephone service.

We are all in this together and as neighbors, we have to work together to create jobs and improve our economies.

MULTI–PRONG APPROACH TO ENERGY DEVELOPMENT

The Navajo Nation prefers a multi-prong approach to capitalize on our energy needs. Several energy options are at our disposal. We balance our economic opportunities with our environmental concerns and take a realistic view of the following energy packages: 1) Renewable Energy: a) wind, b) solar, c) other technologies, and d) extend the production tax credits and investment tax credits which support the growth of renewable energy, 2) A viable future with coal: a) clean coal technology and, b) applying sophisticated best available retrofit technology for existing coal development, and 3) Natural gas fired power plants.

Additionally, we oppose uranium mining on the Navajo Nation reservation. In the same vein, the Navajo Nation opposes any budget cuts to the Surface Mining Control and Reclamation Act (SMCRA) that funds Navajo Nation Abandoned Mine Lands (AML) Reclamation Program.

1) Renewable Energy

We are blessed with an abundance of natural resources including coal, oil and natural gas, as well as renewable resources, such as wind and solar. The Navajo Nation endorses renewable energy resources and embraces a vision for an energy economy that ensures long-term economic and social progress that positively impacts the regional economies of the Four Corner States.

A. WIND GENERATION

The Navajo Nation is working on three sites for utility-scaled wind generation development:

1. **Boquillas Ranch (Seligman, Arizona):** Potential for up to 500 Mega Watt (MW) wind farm. Leases for phase 1A and 1B were approved by the Navajo Nation Council in December 22, 2009, with groundbreaking anticipated in December 2011.

2. **Gray Mountain (Cameron, Arizona):** Potential for up to 500 MW wind farm. Grey Mountain is likely the best wind site on the Nation. We are working with the local community and potential developers to realize this project. We have secured the interconnection queue position to transmit power from this proposed wind farm.
3. **Black Mesa (Kayenta, Arizona):** Potential for up to 200MW wind farm. Preliminary wind data warrants formal wind study at two sites on Black Mesa.

The Navajo Nation is actively exploring other potential wind sites.

B. SOLAR GENERATION

The location of the Navajo Nation (its latitude and elevation) makes it extremely attractive for solar generation development. To accelerate solar development, we are partnering with the U.S. Environmental Protection Agency (USEPA) to assess and prioritize potential sites for solar development.

C. OTHER TECHNOLOGIES

The Navajo Nation is exploring additional technologies such as: waste-to-energy, geothermal, and biomass opportunities available to our Nation.

D. CONGRESS SHOULD EXTEND PRODUCTION AND INVESTMENT TAX CREDITS FOR RENEWABLE ENERGY

The Navajo Nation has benefitted from the American Recovery and Reinvestment Act of 2009, which extends both the production and investment tax credits. Some companies that generate wind, solar, and geothermal energy benefit from the tax credits and are incentivized to develop renewable energy projects on reservation. These tax credits will end in 2013. Congress should renew this legislation today to provide additional time for entrepreneurs to plan ahead so they are able to make investments that promote economic development on the reservation.

CLEAN COAL TECHNOLOGY

A) DESERT ROCK

Desert Rock Energy Project (Desert Rock) is proposed by Sithe Corporation (Sithe) in partnership with Diné Power Authority (DPA), a Navajo Nation Enterprise. Desert Rock is a merchant power plant, meaning that Sithe plans to sell power on the open market and has no current contracts. Sithe has suggested that Desert Rock "off-takers" (buyers of power) include Arizona Public Service, Nevada Power, and the Salt River Project, for energy primarily slated for Tucson/Phoenix and the Las Vegas markets. A small percentage, up to 5%, of the proposed power from Desert Rock would stay on the Navajo Nation, where many citizens continue to live without electricity.

The USEPA issued a Prevention of Significant Deterioration permit in 2008; but remanded the approved permit in 2009. Currently, the permit is under appeal. The denial of the permit has stopped the Desert Rock Project.

Desert Rock will be one of the newest and cleanest coal generating plants in the country. Revenues from Desert Rock will be about one-third of the entire Navajo Budget and will allow us to head towards the path of self-sufficiency. Thousands of construction and high paying full-time jobs will be lost.

B) CURRENT POWER PLANTS NEED TO APPLY SOPHISTICATED BEST AVAILABLE RETROFIT TECHNOLOGY FOR EXISTING COAL DEVELOPMENT

The Navajo Nation seeks a balance between environmental protection to promote human health and economic opportunities supporting job sustainability. It is important for the federal government to make good on its responsibilities to properly consult with the Navajo Nation regarding any policies or decisions that could affect us since these pending Proposed Rules and future Rules could devastate the Energy Industry.

Accordingly, last year the Navajo Nation submitted comments to USEPA regarding the Advance Notice of Proposed Rulemaking: Assessment of Anticipated Visibility of Improvements at Surrounding Class 1 Areas and Cost Effectiveness of Best Available Retrofit Technology (BART) of the Four Corners Power Plant and Navajo Generating Station. The Navajo Nation recommended the following:

a. A phased approach to emissions reductions for the plants, in coordination with the glide path from 2004 to 2064, and
b. Combustion controls—low NO_x burners, or LOX and separated over fire air technology or SOFA, are BART for both Plants at this time (we did not agree to the use of Selective Catalytic Reduction (SCR) technology, and

    c. USEPA should incorporate the use of real, recorded, and available data be used in its decision making instead of relying solely on modeling data, and

    d. USEPA should seriously consider the potential negative impacts to the fragile Navajo Nation economy due to a decision that requires the use of high cost SCR technology.

There are many important considerations that federal agencies, such as the USEPA, must review in light of any rulemaking that may affect the energy development goals of the Navajo Nation. The USEPA has a framework in place to guide government-to-government consultation and policies that consider impacts to Indian lands. The Navajo Nation has provided many of its natural resources for the benefit of its own people and many others throughout the Southwest. We know our coal reserves can continue to supply solid base load electricity, and we know it is important to expand our renewable energy portfolio. We are ready to work side-by-side with you to address and resolve energy demands in our local communities and across the Southwest.

3) NATURAL GAS POWERED POWER PLANTS

The Navajo Nation is looking at all future viable alternatives in energy development. Natural gas generated power plants have limited environmental degradation potential. It's estimated that the Navajo Nation has 25 trillion cubic feet of natural gas. It is one of our top alternative energy resources.

NAVAJO OPPOSES URANIUM MINING

The Dine Natural Resources Protection Act of 2005 is still in effect which essentially bans uranium mining and processing on the Navajo Nation.

We are deeply empathetic to this subject and we stand against uranium mining on the reservation. The Navajo Nation contributes to the energy needs of the American public, however, we still suffer devastating health impacts from uranium mining that took place during World War II efforts.

We are very concerned about the long-term health impacts from uranium that have affected our people and communities. Today, there are still uranium hot spots on the reservation. Some of the abandoned uranium mines even impacts our groundwater resources and our drinking water.

We are asking Congress to do everything possible to continue the scientific research regarding the health impacts and put all federal agencies attached to the World War II efforts on notice to REMEDIATE continued hotspots on the Navajo Nation and to deal with this legacy of government sponsored uranium mining.

I would like to express my appreciation for the Congressional leadership since 2007 to initiate a multi-agency, and a multi-year plan to address the impacts of uranium mining on the Navajo Nation. Working with seven federal agencies, under direct oversight of the Committee of Oversight and Government Reform and the Committee of Energy and Commerce, we are now past the mid-point of a five-year plan. There are a growing number of accomplishments, but one thing is evident—there is still a lot more work to be done to address the many issues, especially the need for more resources for mine assessments, cleanup, and health assessment projects. I look forward to continuing this important effort beyond the scheduled five-year term, which ends in 2012.

NAVAJO AML–CONTINUE FUNDING

In the same vein, the Navajo Nation opposes any budget cuts that go to the Surface Mining Control and Reclamation Act that fund the Navajo Nation AML Reclamation Program. The Navajo AML projects have a fundamental commitment to assure the wellness and safety of the Navajo people by safeguarding abandoned mines and basic vital community infrastructure.

CONCLUSION

The Navajo Nation believes in taking the initiative to be more competitive to fulfill the dynamic demands of social, economic, political and environmental issues. We will continue to collaborate with our partners and neighbors in order to accomplish all of our priorities for this administration.

Aheehe', thank you.

––––––––

Mr. YOUNG. I thank the total panel, and what you are saying is true, and the purpose of this hearing will be, and after we have our questions, we are going to write a piece of legislation, and we want to streamline it, and make sure that you have the opportunity for self-determination that we promised you.

This idea of not being able to do things is wrong. Now, we will have—and I hate to say that it is going to be about an hour, but we have 3 minutes and 16 seconds to go vote, and you guys relax, and do whatever you want to do until we get back.

And we will notify you about five minutes before we are going to reconvene. I want to thank the Committee, and we will see you later.

[Recess.]

Mr. YOUNG. The Committee will come back to order. I do apologize to the witnesses. It is something that we can't control, and we had some very important votes, and so I just do apologize for that and in bearing with us.

But all of the witnesses have testified, and if my good Members can remember what they said, I am going to recognize the Ranking Member at this time to ask questions.

Mr. BOREN. Thank you, Mr. Chairman. I have a few questions, and I am very interested by the testimony. Let me start with Mr. Hall. In North Dakota, and all the things that are going on in the Bakken Shale, in our State of Oklahoma, we actually have a lot of companies that are exploring natural resources there, Continental Resources being one of them, which is based in Eden, Oklahoma.

A lot of jobs, and I noticed that North Dakota has the lowest employment rate in the United States. Could you tell us, and with you in particular, and being Chairman, what is your tribe's unemployment rate compared to the rest of the State?

Mr. HALL. Congressman, we are probably at about 30 percent, and we have a TERO office at our tribal headquarters, and it stands for Tribal Employment Rights Office.

So that office is to make sure that the Indian contractors, or tribal members that want to work on a drilling rig, or work on a production site, are getting those jobs, and then the training. Of course, you have to have training, and a lot of safety H2S, and a lot of certification, because you are dealing with oil and gas, and that sort of thing. So safety is really big, and so we are working with our Tribal College, and so we are starting to make a dent, but we have a way to go.

Mr. BOREN. Well, I think the Chair and I have been talking about how we can streamline the regulatory burden, and how we can work together, obviously by keeping a good environmental record. We want to have a clean environment.

But we also want to give you all the tools to succeed. Mr. Russell, let me ask you a little bit about the ADP fees. With respect to that, what justification if any has the BLM offered to justify the disparity between off and on reservation drilling? And the numbers that were given to me, about $6,500 per well, where it is much, much less on non-Indian land; could you talk to us a little bit about that, and what has BLM said to you all, the Crow Nation, the Crow Tribe?

Mr. RUSSELL. Thank you for the question. Beginning with the Fiscal Year 2008, the Appropriations Act for the Department of the Interior, Congress required the Bureau of Land Management to charge that $4,000 fee. It used to be $4,000.

And it was to process every application for a permit to drill, APD, and on that appropriation, it said Federal and Indian lands which it supervises its oil and gas development activity.

We would need an act of Congress to remove Indian lands from that legislation. We have approached the Bureau of Land Management. They say talk to your Congressman. This is something that most tribes here at the table have to deal with.

And I mentioned earlier that it is a travesty of the system. It just is not right that you take one step off the reservation, and pay a hundred dollars for a test well, where you have to pay 6,500 dollars, and I heard that that price is going up.

Mr. BOREN. Well, thank you for that, and I think we are going to over the next few weeks and months, we are going to look at ways that we can lower some of those fees, or work with you all.

The last question is for Mr. Shelly. Do you foresee when energy is a major area for development by the Navajo Nation going forward, and perhaps signaling a departure from traditional non-renewable energy development? Do you see that as maybe something to look at?

Mr. SHELLY. Yes, we do. We have always believed in our tradition and cultures when we do break ground for any development. There is some—well, when you say traditional energy, meaning maybe coal burning is what you are looking at asking.

We are looking at that, and the only thing that I can tell you is that the Navajo Nation has a lot of coal. We have a 200 year supply of coal. So a lot of Indian tribes, that is all that they have to offer, but we are also learning that new technology in coal is also there to produce liquid fuel from it.

And we are looking at that and to do that. We want to explore that and then use our coal in that way, and it will produce fuel from it, and there are other things that you can make off of it, too.

So we are looking at new things, and not sitting in the old way of just having coal. We are looking at other new things.

Mr. BOREN. Thank you, and thank you, Mr. Chairman, and I yield back.

Mr. YOUNG. Mr. Denham, you are up. Do you have any questions?

Mr. DENHAM. I will yield.

Mr. YOUNG. Mr. Kildee.

Mr. KILDEE. Thank you, Mr. Chairman, and again I join you in apologizing to the panel for our break in the schedule. It happens around here, and I still apologize. I have a question for President Shelly.

President Shelly, I would hope that we could settle all these issues at least as well as we did the Navajo-San Juan Water Settlement, which was signed last December with Interior Secretary Ken Salazar.

Is there anything that we can learn from that water settlement that might help us guide an energy development to help make it less complicated and involve fewer agencies and fewer steps?

Mr. SHELLY. The San Juan water settlement, we went through a lot of problems with that. We have—it is a thing that we are getting a lot of conflicting—the Bureau and the Federal agencies have had a lot to do with that.

We tried to provide what we want in the water settlement, and the water rights, but we were—there is a lot, and it comes right back down to that tribes are regulated and over-regulated in a lot of areas, and this is what we are talking about.

There is so much red tape there that you have to hurdle all of that, and I think the lesson that we learned from that is that if we look at those policies, those Federal policies that hold us down, and not get what we want, and we start being directed toward the Federal programs, they start controlling it, and we lose a lot of that in that way.

And so that is why we are expressing that there is too much red tape, and we need to take care of those Federal regulations that really hinders us all.

Mr. KILDEE. So you found that there are similar difficulties, both like in the water settlements and your energy development?

Mr. SHELLY. It is. It is the same. I believe that water is energy, and it is our hope that Mr. Young here considers water as part of the policy, because water is energy, and all the rest that goes along with it with oil and coal.

So if red tape does happen, that should also be covered in there by the water area. Thank you.

Mr. KILDEE. I think that you make a very good point. I think the Hoover Dam illustrates that water is energy. Hydropower has been something existing early in mankind's development.

So we should probably look at both these areas and try to see what we can do to expedite the water settlement issues, and energy issues then.

Mr. SHELLY. Yes.

Mr. KILDEE. Thank you very much, and I yield back, Mr. Chairman.

Mr. YOUNG. Mr. Gosar, you are next.

Dr. GOSAR. Well, thank you because we are going to make that point right now and tie them together. President Shelly, we are both very concerned about the regulatory uncertainty surrounding the Navajo generating station in Northern Arizona.

The Navajo generating station is essential to the Navajo Nation, providing almost 500 jobs just at the station itself, and then an additional 400 jobs at the Black Mesa Coal Mine in Kayenta.

The station is important because it is the sole source of power for the Central Arizona project, which provides nearly half of the water for the Metropolitan Phoenix area, and approximately 85 percent of the water for the Tucson area, the number five and thirty-second largest cities in the country.

And nearly 90 percent of the water for Pinal County, one of the fastest growing counties in the country. As you mentioned in your testimony, the EPA is expected to issue a final rule on the Bart process in determining how that regional haze rule for the Clean Air Act will be adjudicated.

As you know, this final rule could put an effective end to the Navajo generating station, and put the future of Arizona's water supply process under serious doubt. Couple that with the need for Los Angeles water and power to be out of the equation as a partnership, this provides a lot of uncertainty.

How were you involved with the EPA process, and what hoops did you have to jump through, and how could you look at that process in a little better light?

Mr. SHELLY. Thank you for the question. I know that the Navajo generating station is in renegotiation with the Navajo Nation, and let me make a point here. It is not—what I want to say here in my statement is not the Navajo position.

I cannot position a Navajo position without the Navajo Nation Council being involved. We are still in the negotiation stage, and we are still going through public hearings and so on.

But let me say this. My statement will relate to Navajo interests. I am not stating a position, but this is Navajo interests, and I want to express that. Number one, Navajo interests.

There are three units in the Navajo generating station, and two units have low NO_x, sulfur, and that has been upgraded to that, and the third unit is being shut down to also upgrade the low NO_x.

But we have an issue with the USEPA. The USEPA comes around and says that I want the full upgrade on your emission scrubber, which will cost about a billion dollars, and that is where we get into where our differences come out.

So the SRP are running the plant, and we have met on this, and the SRP and the Navajo Nation are supporting the low NO_x, but the EPA is not. So it is a big concern to us because what everybody is saying is that if SRP goes with the higher cost of scrubber upgrade, we are in the process of negotiation. So it will hurt the fee for the lease that we would be negotiating. So it will be lower. Mainly it is just common sense. If they are going to spend a billion dollars, it will not be there for us to meet what we want for the lease fee.

So that is a big concern to us. That is the Navajo interest that I am expressing to you. So who are the large percentage owners? Yesterday, we have gone to those large percentage owners, and which is 23 percent that is owned by the Department of the Interior.

So we have asked our champion, our trustee, to stand up for us against the USEPA, and to stand up with us to go with the low NO_x emission, and not what the USEPA are saying, the billion dollar upgrade.

So we have asked for that, and those are what we have gone around with yesterday. The other one is that the grass root Navajos that live around the power plant also are saying that we really want to shut down, and we do want to shut down the Navajo generating station.

But when you talk to them, the reason why they are saying that is because there are no improvements around that power plant. Believe it or not, only half a mile from the power plant, there is no running water, and no electricity for these residents. It doesn't make sense.

I believe that as the President that I did talk to the SRP people on what we can do for the grass roots people around there, and they are willing to work with the gross roots residents there, and giving them water and electric.

So that is the compromise that they made, and so there it is. The grass roots concerns have been resolved, and so again here is the thing. We also told the Department of the Interior that you have to create another Federal line item budget, which is going to cost Congress 50 million dollars a year.

Meaning that if you shut down the Navajo generating station, the shareholders, that other tribe in the water area, will lose that funding. So this is why it is a big concern with the shareholders.

They don't want to shut down, and then you go to the State of Arizona, and they also don't want to shut it down. So here we are. We have the USEPA trying to do that. So this is the big thing, and this is why we went to the Department of the Interior, and for them to stand up for us, and take a position here.

And this is a big concern to us, and so the Navajo Nation really does not want to say anything, because we have two tribes that depend on that, and on their survival. The Navajo Nation provides coal to the generating and also the Hopi Tribe.

The Hopi Tribe has 70 percent of their revenue that comes off of coal. Now, if that shuts down, the Hopi Tribe and 70 percent of their revenue will be in jeopardy, and they will be hurting.

And that is the reason why that this is the difference between the USEPA and our position. Thank you.

Mr. YOUNG. We will have another round if you wish. Mr. Luján.

Mr. LUJÁN. Mr. Chairman, thank you very much to you and the Ranking Member for calling this important hearing. Again, welcome to all of our tribal leaders that are here today.

My friend, President Shelly, from the Navajo Nation, again, Mr. President, welcome. Mr. Chairman, I am encouraged by the fact that we are here to be able to have a conversation and to talk about real ways that we can strengthen sovereignty and to work with our Indian brothers and sisters from around the United States.

I think that is an important dialogue that can only be strengthened here in the Congress, and there is no doubt that many of the tribes in our country are uniquely positioned to help our country move forward with energy production, with job creation, especially in areas with natural gas renewables, and other areas where we can see advances made.

And as in this case with the Navajo Nation, tribes that have energy resources will certainly be a part of our country's energy future, and we will need to encourage them to develop energy sources safely and responsibly so that the jobs and revenues created lead to long-term economic stability, and not limit tribes to just developing one resource or another that are finite and may diminish.

And that could potentially have an impact on our people. We have a great opportunity to work with our tribes to help them create jobs for their communities and becoming energy leaders of the future.

And it starts by correcting problems with red tape. I am glad to hear that highlighted so much today. So that as we talk about standardizing the process so that tribes are not at a disadvantage, and to make sure that we have a less complicated and more efficient process, I believe, is what Mr. Hall suggested, which I think is the right approach.

Let me give you an example. Over 90 percent of the Hickory Apache Nation's government, operations are funded with revenues from production of their oil and gas resources.

At least three separate agencies with the Department of the Interior have jurisdiction over Indian leasing; the BIA, the BLM, and the MMS. The Hickory Apache Nation has suffered tremendous losses because they have not been informed of non-compliance by operators and lessees until months or years after non-compliance has occurred.

This is a result of the multiple jurisdictions and a lack of standardized process. When there is non-compliance that is restricting revenues that are yours, that belong to our tribes.

You should be told, so that way you can collect those revenues, and the government has the responsibility to do a better job to assist you and enforcing those policies so that those revenues go to you to help your people, and provide that economic opportunity.

This example shows how tribal nations get left behind because of the bureaucratic process of obtaining leases, permits, and there is no doubt that we need to streamline the process so that tribal nations can be competitive in harnessing the energy for their people, for the entire Nation, and for the betterment of our country.

But let us not forget that we also have a trust responsibility to protect tribal lands from overdevelopment, and bad practices of the energy industry as we have seen in the Gulf, and as we have seen in the development of uranium on the Navajo Nation.

I am proud to say that next week, I will be introducing the RECA Amendments, the Radiation, Exposure, and Compensation Act, which I hope that my colleagues will be willing to support.

This is a responsibility that we have to workers that were impacted, and that have cancer, and kidney failure, and that generations have lost their lives because of the neglect of our Nation in this area.

And it is a responsibility that we have, and it is a responsibility that we must make as part of any energy policy going forward to help our impacted workers all across America, but especially all across Indian Country.

In addition, in streamlining the bureaucratic process, we will need to help our tribal communities train a qualified workforce. This year, in H.R. 1, which passed the House, and in a measure that I opposed, slashed funding for the Navajo Technical College, which is going to devastate technical training for energy jobs in the Nation.

As we talk about developing energy resources, we have to work to make sure that we have adequate training so that you can have all the resources that you need to employ everyone that is unemployed today all across the country.

In addition, we have a piece of legislation that has been introduced by Steve Pearce, a colleague of mine from New Mexico, with SMCRA funding, and this is an area as the President outlined that we have to move forward to make sure that we clean up areas around New Mexico and other parts of the country that deserve to be cleaned up so that neglect is not going to be part of this problem.

Once we get to solving the Nation's problems, and especially problems that we have seen in Indian Country, I think we will be better off and helping to further advance our ability to do this responsibly.

So, Mr. Chairman, I thank you very much. I look forward to asking a few questions in the second round, and again thank you for this important hearing.

Mr. YOUNG. We may not have a second right, and I will tell you that, because we are going to have votes. So remember my good friend that you could have submitted that same statement before, and there were no questions there. Thank you. Just keep that in mind. The good lady from Hawaii.

Ms. HANABUSA. Thank you, Mr. Chairman, and thank you all for being here. I have a question, and I am going to address this to Mr. Russell, because you seem to have the most detailed testimony submitted.

As leases are entered into, and any of the others can step in at any time, but as you negotiate your leases are there any concerns about cultural practices, or sensitivities, that your respective Indian Nations may have as to whether your mining, drilling, or any other form, water retention, anything?

Mr. RUSSELL. Thank you for the question. We perpetuate our culture by how we live it, and similar to the cultures of your State there, before we do anything, we offer prayers.

We feel that all of the elements were provided to us by the creator to use for our benefit, and with some of the things that we are doing right now, we are utilizing the renewable energy.

Right now, we need a lot of help from your part on creating laws and tax incentives to help us. I mentioned in my testimony that once you mention coal, it seems like it is such a dirty word, but it is not.

Coal can be made clean, and we need all the help that we can get when it comes to coal. We need to extend the expiration date of the current 50 cents per gallon of alternative fuel tax credit for at least 10 years.

This will give us enough time to look for more investors so that we can start up these major projects, but I really appreciate your question, especially when it comes to our culture.

Like I mentioned, we live our culture, and we live in two different worlds. I addressed this body in my own language because it was the proper thing to do in my culture. Thank you.

Ms. HANABUSA. Thank you very much, and I noticed that as well, and as you know, in Hawaii, we are going through a very similar process, especially in the alternative energy of geothermal, which is very much tied to the Hawaiian goddess Pele.

And let me also ask you about something that you mentioned, which is also the need for tax credits. One of the things that I was wondering is that as you looked—and I believe in one of your testimonies, it was like 70 percent of the employees were really from the Nation.

But the question is that when you have tax credits are benefitting from the people that you lease to, do you feel that it would be a good time to, in essence, increase the number of the Native people being hired in order to qualify for tax credits, or to get a higher credit some sort so that you can ensure as part of the lease that you get the tax credit, and that in fact your people are being hired, and a preference, or something similar?

Mr. RUSSELL. Yes, of course. You know, we want to hire our own people. With that Indian Coal Tax Production Credit, we need that permanent also, because we rely on it. For our tribal government, and in my testimony, it is written as 40 percent, and it is actually 60 percent and higher.

Two-thirds of our budget comes from the taxes and the lease revenues from coal, and if that is taken away, I don't know what we will do as a government. It is devastating to us. We need those in place, and we need a more permanent—and I do agree with you that we want our own tribal members to excel, and we also want them to—you know, we have the caliber of professionals that have been working there.

This mine has been in existence for 37 years. Our own tribal members are very capable of achieving the status of management, and we are actually shooting for that, and with the new projects that we have, we learn from this mine, and we are actually building capacity with our local school.

We have a tribal school there, and we are actually looking at a total liquids plant, and something fairly new. It is so new that there is no curriculum for that. So we are working on developing that also.

Ms. HANABUSA. Thank you. I am running out of time, but I did want to say, and if you could respond in writing if you don't have enough time, but this whole idea of the liquid coal intrigues me.

And I also sit on our Armed Services, and I think that it was you who mentioned that we need a DoD relationship. So can you expand on that? Are you talking about research and development in the area of liquid coal as jet fuel?

Mr. RUSSELL. Exactly, and we need this body to grant the Department of Defense and other Federal agencies. We need the ability to enter into long-term guaranteed fixed price contracts.

This will help and enable this process, and it will help this project become a reality. You know, we mentioned earlier about the 50 cents per gallon alternative fuel tax. That needs to be in place a lot longer than it is now.

We need those in place so that these people will put their money down. This is proven technology. It has been around for a long time, but it is very costly, but eventually it is a win-win situation for everybody. We could be major contributors to this Nation's energy crisis.

Ms. HANABUSA. Thank you, and my apologies, Mr. Chair, for going over.

Mr. YOUNG. Mr. Denham.

Mr. DENHAM. Thank you, Mr. Chairman. I have a number of different questions, but for the sake of time, because we are getting close to votes, I am going to submit those.

But I did want to get one question out for the record. As I have traveled to a number of different reservations, I have noticed that there has been a challenge in getting large projects done if local governments can bond.

Do you have the ability to bond yourselves, whether it is an energy project, or a community development project?

Mr. HALL. Yes, Congress passed the—what do they call it—the tribal renewable energy bond, TREB, and it was a temporary—I think it was two billion in total was for tribes to finance.

Mr. DENHAM. And is that just for renewable energy, or is that for all energy?

Mr. HALL. I need some clarification on it. I know that it stands for TREB, but I thought it was Tribal Renewable Energy Bond, because I know the acronym stands for TREB.

Mr. DENHAM. And what about other development projects? One in particular that I visited was where they put a new ballpark in, but it was extremely difficult not being able to use a bond for it.

Mr. HALL. Well, your point is well taken. We are trying to put a refinery at Fort Berthold in North Dakota, and we have been waiting for eight years to get EPA our ROD, our record of decision and permit.

And then you get the financing, and you can't get financing until you get your ROD and your permit. It is more of a guaranteed loan. It is a limited offer, and limited support for that from the Department of the Interior. So, no, on the bonding for a clean fields refinery.

Mr. DENHAM. Thank you.

Mr. YOUNG. Mr. Faleomavaega.

Mr. FALEOMAVAEGA. Thank you, Mr. Chairman. I certainly want to commend you and thank you for your leadership. I could not have asked for a better Member to chair this Subcommittee in the years that we have worked together on issues affecting the needs of our Native American and Native Alaskan community.

And thank you again for this hearing, and I always welcome my good friend and brother, Tex Hall, to be here this morning. I was interested and wanted to know, that to your knowledge, gentlemen, has the Department of the Interior ever conducted any surveys or analysis on the amount of oil and natural gas, or other minerals, contained on Indian lands in all the years that we have been together

Mr. SHELLY. No. No, they have not.

Mr. FALEOMAVAEGA. I was wondering, Mr. Chairman, that maybe by way of legislation that this could be something that the Interior Department could do to help our tribes in this regard.

Mr. SHELLY. And, Congressman, just to add to that, but when you are talking about fair market value, it is hard to establish fair market value of your asset if you don't really know what you have, and how much, and how rich that natural gas is, or the type of crude, and whether it is sweet or sour.

So, yes, that is really needed to establish what your asset, your mineral, really is worth, so that you can have the ability to finance and do exploration.

Mr. FALEOMAVAEGA. I want to say to my friend from New Mexico to please put me on as a cosponsor of the proposed legislation of those victims, of the Navajo people and the radiation.

I say this from my own personal experience, in terms of the nuclear testings that we conducted in the Marshall Islands, where several hundred Merciless people were exposed to nuclear contamination, and to this day, we still have not given proper medical treatment to the victims and those people who were exposed to nuclear radiation.

We exploded some 6 to 7 nuclear bombs in the Marshall Islands, and I want to ask President Shelly, I have been to Kazakhstan, and I don't know if you are aware that Australia and Kazakhstan currently produces the vast majority of the amount of uranium supplied in the world.

And I wonder if the Federal Government could do a better job in cleaning up the mess that we created and in harvesting the uranium in your lands, do you think that we still have the amount of reserves of uranium supply on Navajo lands to this day?

Mr. SHELLY. The Navajo are sitting on two-thirds of the finest uranium there is. We are sitting on it. And the cleanup—let me just say this. If you are cutting ALM money, that is the cleanup for all of the open pits that still exist, and there are over a thousand open pits that still exist on the Navajo Nation.

The Navajo Nation passed a law to ban all uranium mining and no discussion, and that is why I stated that earlier, and until that is cleaned up, then maybe the Navajo Nation can change the law that they mandated in prohibiting mining. And they might change it, and sit at the table and talk about uranium.

Mr. FALEOMAVAEGA. No, you said that the mess that was created, was it created by the companies that harvested the uranium, or was it by the Federal Government?

Mr. SHELLY. It was by a company that did it, and they disappeared. We can't find them. Nobody can find them. They are gone. So there it is.

Mr. FALEOMAVAEGA. And have there been any estimates taken in terms of what would it would take to clean up the mess that they caused?

Mr. SHELLY. It is going to be an outrageous amount. I don't have the numbers, but like I said, there was a lot. Now, they took care of some open pit minds, but they are not doing enough of it yet. So with less funding right now, it is not happening. So there are still some mine openings.

Mr. FALEOMAVAEGA. Is it possible that the tribe could consider the possibility of some way or somehow the technology and all of that? I say this because if it was possible for Australia and Kazakhstan to produce the majority of the amount of uranium supplies—we have 104 nuclear reactors in our own country, and I am sure that there is a need for uranium.

And I cannot believe that you still have two-thirds of the reserves that have not been harvested, and I am just curious. With the technology and the proper review, is there some way or somehow that this could be done.

I know that my time is up, Mr. Chairman, but I definitely would like to pursue that further with you, Mr. Russell. Thank you, Mr. Chairman.

Mr. YOUNG. I want to thank the panel. My suggestion is—and I don't have a lot of questions, but I would just ask each one of you—I know your testimony is good, and I am sure that you have legal-beagles around somewhere, and we are going to write a bill.

And from what we have heard here today, the roadblocks, and what I call the two-step, and you take two steps forward, and three steps back. And it is really caused by the Federal Government.

We know where you have not been able to go because of that, and so I am suggesting that when we write this bill that you submit what you think should be done. Personally, I would like to see you have the total responsibility for all your resource development.

Why should we shift it through three different agencies. Did you say 49 different permit requirements?

Mr. HALL. Yes, 49 steps for leasing.

Mr. YOUNG. Yes, for leasing, and the drain on you and for making it non-attractive is very evident. So any ideas on—and one last question for you, Mr. Russell. Did you say that they condemned land on your reservation to build a dam, and you have never been reimbursed for it?

Mr. RUSSELL. That is correct. Fifty-five hundred acres were condemned and a dam was built, and in the 50 years that that dam has been in existence, the government has made 600 million dollars.

Originally when it was first built, I believe that they gave the Crow Tribe about 3 to 5 million, somewhere around there. Either way, it was not very substantial.

Mr. YOUNG. I hate to ask this question, but was that condemned by the Congress, or was that condemned by a utility?

Mr. RUSSELL. That was condemned by the Federal Government.

Mr. YOUNG. By the Federal Government, and the BIA did not say anything?

Mr. RUSSELL. No, apparently not.

Mr. YOUNG. OK. Well, we will review that. I have already said that Pallone is not going to ask any questions of this group. I mean, you can on the next one. Those that are late don't get any bait. But we did say you could sit here and we did make that perfectly clear. Yes, Doctor? I mean, Ben?

Mr. SHELLY. Chairman Young, on Monday, I will have a legal beaver on this, and let me ask you in front of all of the panel here, the Navajo Nation will take part in this, and help along.

I think that all of us agreed earlier that we want our input in helping you with the bill.

Mr. YOUNG. And we look forward to doing that, too, because I say that this is a great time to raise the ability for the tribes to take and achieve the goals that they should.

And you have been precluded from that by very frankly big daddy with his hand on your head, saying don't really get too far, and don't get too smart, and don't get too healthy, and don't be self-reliant on yourself. We will take care of you.

And it has not worked, and this is many, many years of I think very poor management, and I don't blame anybody. I have been under eight Presidents, and 13 different Secretary of the Interiors. You can check it out, and the BIA is the bottom of the barrel.

It always has been, and so I don't blame Echo Hawk, or anybody else for what they can't do. What I want to make sure is that you can do it at a later time, and I hope that this Committee will agree with me, and that we can have a great piece of legislation that will solve a lot of our problems.

I want to thank the group, and if the next panel would come up, and you did put your hat back on, sir, and that is a good idea, but I usually ask you to bare your head, but you did good.

Mr. HALL. Thank you, Chairman.

Mr. YOUNG. The next panel is Irene Cuch of the Ute Tribe of the Uintah and Ouray Reservation, and Michael Connolly, Laguna Resources Services, and Neal McCaleb, a good old friend of mine. So everybody take their seats, please.

And at this time, when everybody gets settled down, I will ask my good friend, the Ranking Member, Mr. Boren, to make the introduction of his witnesses.

Mr. BOREN. Well, I wanted to say a special welcome to Neal McCaleb of the Chickasaw Nation. Neal is a household name in Oklahoma. He is also—I see him quite often, not in person, but on television. He stars in a lot of ads right now on the importance of water.

And so we are proud to have him. He has served in the Oklahoma Legislature since 1974 until 1983, and in the spirit of bipartisanship, he was a Republican when he served there in the Legislature.

He has been the Secretary of Transportation in two different administrations at the State level, and he has also been president of the Oklahoma Good Roads and Transportation Association.

And he has been the director of the BIA, and so he has got a unique perspective; the State, the Federal, and all in between. He is going to talk to us, I think, a little bit about natural gas and what is going on with the Chickasaw Nation. So, Neal, welcome, and thank you for your service.

Mr. YOUNG. I thank the gentleman. I knew Neal when he had black hair, too. So I think you all know the rules. Five minutes. Watch that little red button, and then we will have a round of questions, and we will start out with, I believe, Irene. Irene, you are first.

STATEMENT OF IRENE CUCH, MEMBER, BUSINESS COMMITTEE, UTE TRIBE OF THE UINTAH AND OURAY RESERVATION, ACCOMPANIED BY MANUEL MYORE, DIRECTOR, UTE ENERGY AND MINERALS DEPARTMENT

Ms. CUCH. First of all, I would like to say Maiku, and that means greetings in Ute, and Ita vite, which means good day. I just wanted to say this. Chairman Young, and Ranking Member Boren, and Members of the Subcommittee on Indian and Alaska Native Affairs, my name is Irene Cuch, and I am a member of the Ute Tribe Business Committee of the Uintah and Ouray Reservation, which is located in the State of Utah.

Mr. Chairman, if Indian tribes are going to make any progress economically, we need to be allowed to develop our own resources on our own lands. The fact is that a combination of outdated laws, and unhelpful Federal bureaucracy, and environmental extremism, has served to keep Indian tribes from moving ahead with all manner of energy projects.

These include wind farms, as well as coal-fired electrical plants. My testimony will focus on issues that are of paramount importance to the Ute Indian Tribe relating to the tribes energy development on the reservation.

I would like to mention that I also have submitted written testimony to this Subcommittee, and I would like to have this written testimony included and made part of the official record of this hearing.

By the way, I forgot, but I would like to introduce Manuel Myore, who is sitting next to me. He is the Director of Energy and Minerals Resource Department for the Ute Tribe.

By the way of background, the Ute Indian Tribe has 3,157 tribal members living on one of the largest Indian reservations in the United States, with more than 4.15 million acres.

The tribe consists of three Ute Bands, the Uintah, the White River, and the Uncompahgre Bands. The Business Committee has six members, two representatives from each of the three Bands, each of whom serves a four year term.

The tribes mineral estate is comprised of a fractionated checkerboard system of ownership, which makes the regulation and development of the Tribe's natural resources much more difficult.

The Ute Tribe is one of the largest energy producing tribes in the United States. It is estimated that over 5,000 new oil and gas wells will be drilled on the reservation over the next 15 years, involving over 4,600 different proposed surface locations.

The primary source of revenue for the Tribe's government is revenue derived from oil and gas development, making the need to economically extract oil and gas resources on the reservation in an efficient manner of critical importance to the Tribe and its membership.

The Tribe needs at least 450 permit approved by the Bureau of Indian Affairs each year to fully develop its oil and gas resources. Currently, the BIA only approves four APDs per month, which equates to only 10 percent of the permits the tribe needs to meet the needs of industry to optimize the development on tribal lands with energy operators.

Our private sector energy partner routinely indicates that the processing and approval of permits by the agencies is the biggest risk factor in their entire operation on the reservations, and agencies current capacity limitations have served to cut off the revenue stream to the tribe, which limits the tribes' ability to provide critical services and resources to our tribal members.

In the coming years the need for greater regulatory efficiency in the permitting process will become a matter of even greater importance for the Ute Tribe and other energy producing tribes.

Currently, we are working with industry partners, energy minerals, and the Department of the Interior, to secure more funding and staff for tribal and BIA agencies to streamline an increased oil and gas permitting process.

Other inhibitors include the split estate issue, the triggering of the Natural Environmental Policy Act, NEPA, simply by virtue of the Secretary of the Interior's review and approval of leases and other documents, as well as a regulatory gap that currently exists with regard to the Clean Air Act and stationary sources in Indian Country.

In 2005 the Tribe reached agreement with the State of Utah's School and Institutional Trust Lands Authority, SITLA, that would have SITLA relinquish certain mineral interests within the boundaries of the reservation to the tribe and, in turn, SITLA would select other Federal mineral interests also within the boundaries of the reservation.

Once accomplished, the transaction will unify the Tribe's estate in an area of the reservations that is culturally and environmentally sensitive, and one where the Tribe will refrain from oil and gas development.

The subsurface mineral interests to be conveyed to SITLA will also unify its estate in an area that is already subject to oil and gas development.

Mr. YOUNG. Your light is red. You are about ready to run out of time.

Ms. CUCH. OK. I have one minute, right?

Mr. YOUNG. No, you are one minute over.

Ms. CUCH. OK. I am over, but I almost got it done. OK. I just would like to say in closing that I would like to thank Chairman Young, Ranking Member Boren, and Members of the Subcommittee for the opportunity to present these issues on behalf of the Tribe, and can commit to this Subcommittee continued cooperation of the Tribe in finding ways to eliminate these barriers that are preventing the Tribes and the Members from realizing the importance of approved standards of living and our hopes for our children and grandchildren. And at this time, I would like to say Tog'oiak', thank you.

[The prepared statement of Ms. Cuch follows:]

Statement of Irene C. Cuch, Ute Tribal Business Committee Member, Ute Indian Tribe of the Uintah and Ouray Reservation

I. Introduction

Good morning, Chairman Young, Ranking Member Boren, and Members of the Subcommittee on Indian and Alaska Native Affairs. My name is Irene Cuch and I am a member of the Ute Tribal Business Committee of the Uintah and Ouray Reservation, which is located in the State of Utah. First, let me say that the re-establishment of this Subcommittee is a development that Indian Country welcomes and will ensure Indian issues receive the attention they deserve. I would also like to thank the Subcommittee for holding this Oversight Hearing and for providing the Ute Indian Tribe with the opportunity to appear here today. My testimony will focus on issues of paramount importance to the Ute Indian Tribe relating to the Tribe's energy development on the Reservation.

II. Background on the Ute Indian Tribe

By way of background, the Ute Indian Tribe (Tribe) has 3,157 tribal members living on one of the largest Indian reservations in the United States, with more than 4.5 million acres. The Tribe consists of three Ute Bands: the Uintah, the Whiteriver and the Uncompahgre Bands. The Business Committee has six members, two representatives from each of the three Bands—each of whom serves a four year term. The Tribe's mineral estate is comprised of a fractionated, checkerboard system of ownership which makes the regulation and development of the Tribe's natural resources much more difficult. The Tribe's reservation is comprised of the following types of land ownership: Ute Indian Tribe Land, Ute Indian Allotted Land, Ute Distribution Corporation Jointly Managed Indian Trust minerals, along with privately owned fee and federal minerals. Indian Trust lands comprise approximately 1.2 million surface acres, and 1 million mineral acres within the 4.5 million acre reservation boundary. This lack of unity between the mineral and surface estates is an ongoing challenge for the Tribe in developing its mineral resources.

III. Oil and Gas Development Crucial to Tribe's Economy and Government

The tribal government is an important provider of services to the tribal members, managing 60 separate tribal departments and agencies including land, fish and wildlife management, housing, education, emergency medical services, public safety, and energy and minerals management. The primary source of revenue for these tribal departments and agencies is revenue derived from oil and gas development, making the need to economically extract oil and gas resources on the reservation in an efficient manner of critical importance to the Tribe and its membership.

Energy development has long been an important part of our Reservation's economy. Early on in this country's history, as settlers migrated west and began to populate the Tribe's aboriginal areas, the federal government established the Uintah Valley Reservation in 1861 and removed the three bands from their homelands in Colorado to what were thought to be barren lands in the Uintah Basin. But oil was discovered in the Basin and within the Reservation. The early production of oil and gas on the Reservation began in the late 1940's, and further development increased in the 1960's, with significant expansion taking place in the 1970's, 1980's and again today. A significant amount of conventional oil and gas deposits have been explored and developed, and multiple oil and gas operating companies are proposing to continue development of oil and natural gas resources across the Reservation over the next 15 years.

Oil and gas development is important to the Tribe for many reasons, not least of which is because the State of Utah completely prohibits gaming of any kind, and the tribes in Utah do not have the gaming-as-development option. As a result, the Tribe's primary source of income is from oil and gas. The measured economic success of the Tribe has been directly attributable to the development of the Tribe's oil and gas resources. The Tribe has approximately 2,500 wells that include 300 gas wells. Ute tribal lands produce an average of 10,000 barrels of oil per day and we are in the process of opening up an additional 150,000 acres of mineral leases on the reservation with an $80 million investment dedicated to exploration.

To attract outside capital and to assist in the measured development of its energy resources, in 2005, the Tribe established the Ute Energy LLC (Ute Energy). To-date, Ute Energy, which is a majority Ute Tribally owned company, has worked with private equity and energy companies to explore for and develop the Tribe's oil and gas resources. Ute Energy has proven an valuable asset in the Tribe's development, and has plans to drill and operate 54 wells in 2011, with an annual capital budget of $216 million dollars. Through this company, the Tribe has taken an active role in the development of its resources and is investing significant capital and resources into the local economy to generate further development on tribal lands.

Ute Energy has also served the Tribe in generating investment and operational confidence in private sector operators. As an example, in June 2008, the Tribe though Ute Energy teamed with the Anadarko Petroleum Corporation to establish a jointly own the Chipeta gas processing and delivery plant in the Uintah Basin.

Using revenues from energy development, the Tribe has become a major employer and engine for economic growth in northeastern Utah with a diverse array of tribal businesses including a bowling alley, a supermarket, gas stations, a feedlot, an information technology company, a manufacturing plant, Ute Oil Field Water Services LLC, and Ute Energy LLC, an oil and gas development company. Our governmental programs and tribal enterprises employ 450 people, 75% of whom are tribal members. In addition, each year the Tribe generates tens of millions of dollars in economic activity to surrounding towns and communities.

IV. Indian Tribal Energy Has Enormous Potential

As you are aware, Indian tribes throughout this country own a substantial amount of untapped energy resources. Energy production from tribal lands equals ten percent of the total federal onshore production of energy minerals.[1] Indian-owned energy resources are still largely undeveloped: 1.81 million acres are being explored or in production, but about 15 million more acres of energy resources are undeveloped.[2]

There are over 90 tribes that own significant energy resources—both non-renewable and renewable in this country, and it is the goal of all of these tribes to fully develop these resources to provide jobs and incomes to their members and others,

---

[1] Tribal Energy Self Sufficiency Act and Native American Energy and Self Determination Act: Hearing on S. 424 and S. 522 Before the S. Comm. On Indian Affairs, 108 Cong. app. at 93 (2003) (statement of Theresa Rosier, Counselor to the Assistant Secretary-Indian Affairs, U.S. Dep't of the Interior).

[2] See id. (Statement of Sen. Ben Nighthorse Campbell, Chairman, S. Comm. on Indian Affairs).

and to generate revenues to fund the essential programs and activities of tribal governments. Unfortunately, these tribes have quite often been prevented from realizing this goal, and a substantial amount of these energy resources have not been developed because of a number of comparative disadvantages including bureaucratic red tape, physical access limits to pipelines, transmission grids and the financial capital that would allow tribes to be equal partners in the development of their natural resources.

Given the disparate impact these issues have had on reservation economies, the Tribe is encouraged to see that this Subcommittee is holding this hearing to bring attention to these issues, and hopefully will be proposing solutions so that tribes can move forward in the development of their energy resources.

V. Federal Regulatory Impediments Strangle Tribal Development

The Tribe's success in creating economic growth has been curtailed by problems inherent in the federal regulatory system. These regulatory obstacles include delays with the Bureau of Indian Affairs' and Bureau of Land Management's approval of Rights of Ways and Applications for Permission to Drill (APDs), respectively, which serve to limit energy development on the Reservation.

Other inhibitors include the split estate issue, the triggering of the National Environmental Policy Act (NEPA) simply by virtue of the Secretary of the Interior's review and approval of lease and other documents, as well as a regulatory gap that currently exists with regard to the Clean Air Act and stationary sources in Indian Country.

V1. Split Estate Issues as a Major Challenge to Energy Development

Since statehood, the Tribe's Reservation has been checkerboarded with the Tribe, the state and the federal government owning various surface and subsurface interests. The Chairman is familiar with this as a similar situation exists in Alaska with the Regional Corporations owning the subsurface interests and the Village Corporations owning the surface interests.

In 2005, the Tribe reached agreement with the State of Utah's School and Institutional Trust Lands Authority (SITLA) that would have SITLA relinquish certain mineral interests within the boundaries of the Reservation to the Tribe and, in turn, SITLA would select other federal mineral interests also within the boundaries of the Reservation.

Once accomplished, the transaction will unify the Tribe's estate in an area of the Reservation that is culturally and environmentally sensitive and one where the Tribe will refrain from oil and gas development. The subsurface mineral interests to be conveyed to SITLA will also unify its estate in an area that is already subject to oil and gas development.

This is the kind of "win-win" agreement that we think makes a lot of sense, and will also result in American energy development at a time when it is critical that we develop our own resources.

Since 2006, a petition to effectuate this agreement has been pending with the U.S. Department of the Interior. Despite the unanimous support of the Tribe, the State of Utah, and Duchesne, Grand, and Uintah Counties, the department has failed to review or approve the petition, claiming it lacks the legal authority to do so.

The Tribe and the State of Utah disagree with the department's legal analysis but, nonetheless, have agreed to seek a legislative clarification of the legal authority. On March 11, 2011, Representative Jim Matheson introduced H.R. 1053, co-sponsored by Representative Rob Bishop.

The Tribe strongly supports H.R. 1053 and is very appreciative of the determination and support of Mr. Matheson and Mr. Bishop in pursuing this matter. We are, of course, very glad the legislation was referred to this Subcommittee, Mr. Chairman, where we are hopeful it will get a warm welcome and be expedited to the Full Committee and the Floor of the House.

VII. Delays in Approving Applications for Permits to Drill (APDs)

On Reservation, there is a direct correlation between the number of APDs approved and the revenues that are available to the Tribe to fund critical government programs and services. The Tribe has experienced significant delay in the approval of APDs and the agency needs to be more diligent and effective in approving these APDs. While the BLM approves and issues the actual APD for each well, the BIA approves the necessary Right of Way associated with each APD. The Tribe has been made aware that BLM has 90 employees working on APD-related issues, including federal and Indian lands, and approves twice as many APDs as APD associated ROW and NEPA review at the BIA. The BIA has only four people working on these issues at the Uintah and Ouray Agency. As a result, the BIA has not been able to approve the Tribe's APD associated rights of way and NEPA reviews in a timely fashion.

The Tribe estimates that it will need 600–800 Rights of Way Applications processed and approved each year, for the next several years, yet currently the Tribe's energy partners expect 200 such approvals or less at the current rate. Some of these applications have been pending for more than five years, at great cost to the Tribe. As these Rights of Ways and APDs languish, the Environmental Assessments that accompany them become outdated, which results in additional costs to the Tribe. Our private sector energy partners routinely indicate that the processing and approval of permits by the agencies is the biggest risk factor in their entire operation on the Reservation, and the agency's current capacity limitations have served to cut-off the revenue stream to the Tribe, which limits the Tribe's ability to provide critical services and resources to our tribal members.

Put simply, the APD delays have been driving development away from tribal lands in favor of state and private lands with vastly lower associated fees. A real-world example of this disincentive will demonstrate my point. When oil or gas companies bring in drilling rigs without the necessary permits approved, the companies seek other opportunities and the rigs are relocated to other federal, state and private lands. Anadarko, for instance, needs 23 well locations approved per month in 2011 and beyond, but in 2010, their APDs had been approved at a rate of 1.7 per month." Operators, such as Anadarko and others, have indicated that inconsistent approvals of ROWs application result in difficult changes to operation plans and often results in development elsewhere, such as State and private lands. With consistent and reliable ROW and APD approvals, the Tribe is hopeful additional rigs will move on to Tribal lands and increase economic prosperity.

VIII. The National Environmental Policy Act and Tribal Operations

Current law requires the Secretary of the Interior to review and approve leases of Indian land for purposes of mineral development. Since the 1972 Tenth Circuit decision in *Morton v. Davis,* this review and approval has been considered to be a "major federal action" triggering the procedural requirements of the National Environmental Policy Act (NEPA).

As the Subcommittee can imagine, the sheer size of the Tribe's Reservation and oil and gas operations means that the Secretary is asked to review and approve a large number of leases, lease renewals and other business agreements related to mineral development.

As is the case with the APD delays and other associated regulatory challenges, the Tribe witnesses additional delays and cost in having to comply with the NEPA, while energy exploration and development operations on private lands do not. While each of these inhibitors by themselves may not be fatal to tribal development plans, taken together they present a formidable—and almost insurmountable—mountain of challenges. At the end of the day, leases and other required permits that go unapproved or are delayed mean that tribal communities remain mired in poverty and poor economic conditions.

IX. The Regulatory Process Needs to be Streamlined

The Uintah Basin is a prolific producer of oil and gas and the Tribe needs the assistance of the Executive Department, specifically the Assistant Secretary of Indian Affairs, to ensure that the Department of the Interior resolves these backlogs to fulfill its trust responsibility by retaining the necessary personnel within BIA to assist in the APD approval process.

Because of the so-called "49 steps" the BIA has in place to approve energy leases and other business agreements involving many offices within the Bureau, the Tribe believes it would be a prime candidate for establishing a "one stop shop" to resolve these issues concerning the review and approval of leases and APDs, provided that sufficient personnel and funding is authorized and appropriated on a continued basis as necessary to accomplish this effort. The local BIA Agency would need as many as thirty-six additional staff members to process the 40 plus permits per month to meet our needs. In coming years, the need for greater regulatory efficiency in the permitting process will become even more urgent. Based on a survey of the Tribe's operating oil and gas partners conducted as part of the development of the Tribe's Reservation-wide EIS, it is estimated that over 5,000 new wells will be drilled on the Reservation over the next 15 years, involving over 4,600 different proposed surface locations. The creation of a "one-stop shop" designed to improve and streamline the permitting process would greatly benefit the Tribe by allowing for more efficient and effective future management of the Tribe's oil and gas resources.

47

X. Clean Air Act Regulatory Imbalance in Indian Country

Apart from permitting and split estate issues, environmental regulatory issues also are of critical importance to the Tribe. Because the Environmental Protection Agency (EPA) has no Minor Source Permitting Program within Indian Country, gas compressor stations and other stationary sources related to energy development that would normally qualify as a "minor source" under state law and under EPA's own regulations applicable to BLM and other federal lands have been subject to much costlier and more stringent "major source" regulations for purpose of air emissions regulated under the current EPA regulations. This results in a regulatory scheme that is not only fundamentally unfair and inequitable, but which detracts from future energy development in Indian Country, where operators would prefer to locate their energy production facilities on state lands, where such facilities are regulated as "minor source" emitters not major source emitters. Again, this is an instance of a federally-imposed comparative disadvantage that works against tribal development for tribes and their members.

The Tribe has objected to EPA's treatment of minor emitting sources as "major sources" for purpose of air emission regulation given the fact that the application of these major source regulations has created a significant economic disincentive for the Tribe's energy partners and operators to develop tribal minerals on tribal land. The application of these "major source" regulations has had a disastrous effect on the Tribe's energy development on the reservation, as operators instead choose to locate their energy production facilities on state lands, where such facilities are regulated as "minor source" emitters not major source emitters.

The Ute Tribe has therefore led an initiative, in coordination with the Council of Energy Resource Tribes (CERT), of which the Ute Tribe is a charter member, and the National Congress of American Indians (NCAI), to secure support for EPA's issuance of this rule. This would encourage additional energy production on Indian reservations by essentially leveling the playing field for energy development, instituting a comparable system of environmental regulation under federal law that is equal to state environmental regulatory systems.

However, the Tribes have recently been informed that EPA plans to issue this final rule without any further consultation with the affected Tribes. None of the Tribes have been provided with a copy of the Rule, and we are unable to determine what effect it might have on the course of our energy development. However, if the proposed rule does not allow for more efficient and productive environmental regulation of the air shed in Indian Country, or otherwise serves to replace one complex and burdensome set of air permitting regulations with another to the further delay the regulatory process, this rule will have devastating consequences to the Tribes energy development. It is therefore critical that EPA provide the Ute Indian Tribe and other energy producing Tribes with an additional opportunity for review, comment and input on the terms of the proposed rule prior to final approval and promulgation. It is the opinion of the Tribe that EPA's approval and issuance of this rule without further consultation is violative of EPA' trust responsibility to the Ute Indian Tribe and is inconsistent the express terms of EPA's current and proposed consultation policy with Indian Tribes. Many of the problems that have come to arise with Tribal energy development have occurred because Federal Regulatory Agencies to not provide proper consultation with Tribes, and I greatly hope that this proposed minor source rule will not end up as another representative example of this type of problem. President Obama has issued a November 5, 2009 Executive Memorandum, recognizing the need for these Agencies to engage in full and meaningful consultation with Tribes on a government-to-government basis, which included holding subsequent rounds of consultation in situations such as the present one, where there are significant changes in EPA's originally-proposed activity when new issues arise and in providing follow-up consultation giving affected Tribes feedback with regard to how their input has been considered in the final agency action.

In closing, I would like to thank Chairman Young, Ranking Member Boren and members of the Subcommittee for the opportunity to present these issues on behalf of the Tribe and can commit to the Subcommittee the continued cooperation of the Tribe in finding ways to eliminate these barriers that are preventing the Tribe and its members from realizing improved standards of living and hope for our children and grandchildren.

Towaok (Thank You)

UTE INDIAN TRIBAL BUSINESS COMMITTEE

Richard Jenks, Jr., Chairman
Frances M. Poowegup, Vice-Chairman
Irene C. Cuch, Member
Phillip Chimburas, Member

Stewart Pike, Member
Ron Wopsock, Member

For further information contact: (435) 722–5141 or by FAX: (435) 722–5072 Email: businesscommittee@utetribe.com

————

Mr. YOUNG. Thank you. Neal, you are next.

STATEMENT OF NEAL McCALEB, MEMBER, CHICKASAW NATION

Mr. McCALEB. Thank you very much. Mr. Chairman, and Ranking Member Boren, I want to thank you very much for that kind introduction. I am very pleased to have this opportunity to testify to this Committee this afternoon on the use of compressed natural gas in Indian Country as an alternative fuel for vehicles.

I represent the Chickasaw Nation as a member of the Tribe, and serve as Chairman of the Board of the Chickasaw Nation Industries, and as a board member of the Chickasaw wholly-owned bank, and then as an advisor to Governor Anoatubby on economic development issues.

In that respect, the Chickasaws, who are very environmentally sensitive, and market driven in their business decisions, have embarked on a program to migrate our 600 owned and leased vehicles from regular, unleaded fuel to compressed natural gas.

We have constructed, and have operational, our first publicly accessible fast-fill CNG station at our fuel plaza in Ada, Oklahoma, and we are planning to open several more. We have several fuel plazas along the I-35 corridor, and along U.S. 70 across the southern tier of counties in southern Oklahoma.

And this is being done, by the way, without any outside financial assistance. It is being paid for entirely by the Chickasaw Nation, and we are unable to take any tax credits, and so it is all coming out of our jeans.

Our first car purchase was a Honda Civic, which I drove for a period of more than a year. That car has a dedicated CNG engine, meaning that it won't burn anything but compressed natural gas.

And I can tell you that it gave me some operating anxiety and while knuckle trips, and it is a long way between CNG fast fill stations, and when you get to some of them, they are not operational.

And when you are out of gas in a CNG vehicle, you are out of gas. You have just got to call a tow truck to take you to the next CNG station. That is because there is a limited number of convenient fueling stops.

So it is far better to have a "bi-fuel" vehicle. That is a car which will burn both CNG and regular unleaded gasoline, so that if you run out of CNG, you have enough gas to get you to the next CNG station.

Unfortunately, the Federal tax policy does not support that position. There is a tax credit for dedicated CNG engines, cars which happen to be of a foreign make, Honda. There is no tax credit for a bi-fuel engine, which is a lot more practicable in operation than a dedicated engine at this point until we get more conveniently located CNG stations.

The Oklahoma tax code by the way gives a full tax credit for both dedicated engines and bi-fuel engines. Another problem is the EPA certification process, which it seems to me to be designed to delay and confound the process of CNG conversions, and it needs to be streamlined and expedited.

We purchased last year five Chevy Impalas, and had them converted to a bi-fuel/CNG system that cost 10,000 per vehicle, but we had to wait six months after we placed the order for the cars before the EPA would certify the kits for the conversion.

And finally I want to make the point that there is an inequitable treatment of tribes in the Federal Government's efforts to incentivize the use of alternative fuels. Congress has established a 50 cent per gallon fuel excise tax credit or rebate to sellers of qualified alternative fuels. Everybody but tribes, that is.

The credit goes to governments—local, county, city—but not to tribes, and I think that is the point of this hearing, is that Indian tribes are left out either by exception or just forgotten.

And this can be easily remedied by just adding the term into the appropriate legislation "and tribal governments". Again, thank you. I want to thank you and commend you, Congressman Boren, for the legislation that you introduced last year, the Natural Gas Act, which addressed many of these issues.

We very much appreciate it. It is my understanding that you made introduce similar legislation this year, which will be in wholehearted support of. Thank you for the privilege of being here.

[The prepared statement of Mr. McCaleb follows:]

Statement of Neal McCaleb, Member, Chickasaw Nation, and Chairman of the Board, Chickasaw Nation Industries

Good morning. My Name is Neal McCaleb and I want to thank you Chairman Young and Ranking Member Boren for the opportunity to testify before this committee on the subject of energy policy and the use of compressed natural gas (CNG) in Indian country as an alternative fuel for vehicles.

I represent the Chickasaw Nation as a member of the Tribe and serve as Chairman of the Board of Chickasaw Nation Industries, as a board member of its wholly owned bank and as an economic development advisor to Gov. Bill Anoatubby.

The Chickasaws are very environmentally sensitive as well as market driven in our business decisions. We have embarked on a program to migrate our fleet of 600 owned and leased vehicles to CNG fuel and have constructed our first operational public CNG fast fuel station at our fuel plaza in Ada, OK. We are planning to open several more public fast fuel CNG stations at our fuel plazas along I–35 and US 70 in southern Oklahoma.

We have been motivated to make these investments by our desire to provide leadership helping shape energy policy and enhance the national security by becoming less dependent on foreign oil. We respect the need to enhance air quality by reducing vehicle emissions using clean burning natural gas which reduces undesirable emissions including Nitrous Oxide—60% reduction, Carbon Dioxide—30%, Hydrcarbon—50% and particulate matter 90%. Natural Gas burns cleaner than any other energy source except electricity and if you count the carbon footprint to generate the steam powered electricity it burns as clean.

As responsible businessmen we are very interested in the economy of using CNG especially in today's market where low octane fuel is currently at between $3.50 and $4.00/gallon. The cost of an equivalent gallon of CNG varies from $0.75 to $1.39/gallon depending on the point and source of purchase. My personal experience in driving a CNG Chevy conversion for 20,000 miles is that my fuel costs are 3 ½ cents per mile as compared to $0.21/mile for a conventionally fueled car getting 16 miles/gallon at a fuel cost of $3.50/gallon.

These facts coupled with the huge and expanding reserves of natural gas gives a dependable domestic source that will meet the energy needs of this country well into the next century.

The obvious question is "with all these advantages and benefits of CNG what is holding the nation back from a transition to this clean burning, dependable and economic fuel for vehicles?"

I will try an answer from the Chickasaw experience.

First is the supply and demand relationship to the availability of vehicles and fueling opportunities and the demand for the fuel from existing operators. Natural gas vehicles are the fastest growing alternatives to gasoline and diesel around the world—with over 12 million on the road. America has only about 110,000. Around the world, although every major car manufacturer offers natural gas models, currently there are no domestic original equipment manufacturers of CNG cars and until recently only one internationally. With a very limited number of vehicles on the road there is little demand for fueling stations that cost up to $500,000 for one pump without any site development expenses. This is a classic "chicken or egg" conundrum. We can't get more vehicles on the road until there are convenient and reliable fuel stops and the fuel stops won't be developed until there is a demonstrable demand.

The Chickasaws decided to provide leadership by purchasing CNG vehicles and building a local CNG fuel plaza with no financial assistance from any one. Our first car purchase was a Honda Civic that has a "dedicated " engine meaning it burns only CNG. I personally operated this vehicle for a year with no small anxiety about running out of fuel between known fueling locations that I found sometimes were out of service. When you run out of CNG in a dedicated engine car your only option is to call a tow service and be transported to an available fueling site.

In light of the limited number of convenient fueling stops it is far better to have a car that can be powered by either unleaded gas or CNG known as "bi-fuel". There are no original-equipment-manufacturers that produce bi-fuel, natural gas vehicles in the US, and the only viable bi-fuel cars are conversions. We purchased five Chevy Impalas last year and had them converted to bi-fuel at a cost of $10,000/vehicle. We had to wait six months for the EPA to provide the necessary certifications for the make, model and year of the car to be converted. The reason there are no OEMs is that there has been no federal tax credits eligible for bi-fuel cars. There are for single source dedicated cars—but they expired on December 31, 2010. This makes no sense in our current environment of limited fueling opportunities. The more reasonable course for promoting CNG use is to have equal tax credits for both dedicated and bi-fuel cars as we do in under the Oklahoma tax code. Under these conditions there will be greater demand for the bi-fuel cars and subsequently more demand for new and convenient fuel stops.

Secondly the EPA certification process is designed to delay and confound the process of CNG conversions and needs to be streamlined and expedited so that when new models are available the certifications are as well. Under existing rules, each new make and model must be recertified annually as well as the conversion kits. According to Richard Kolodziej, President of NGV America, "currently, the EPA certification process for natural gas aftermarket conversion is cumbersome and unnecessarily costly."

Third, there is an inequitable treatment of tribes in the federal government's efforts to incentivize the use of alternative fuels, including CNG. Congress has established an Alternative Fuels Excise Tax Credit that provides a $0.50/gallon tax credit for sellers of qualifying alternative fuels. Tax-exempt entities such as states and local governments that dispense qualifying fuels from on-site fueling stations to vehicles are eligible for this tax credit. Tribal governments are not eligible. Mr. Chairman this is an issue that comes right to the point of today's hearing. As is so often the case in programs across the federal government, tribes are often simply overlooked and forgotten when legislation and implementing regulations are drafted. The Alternative Fuel Excise Tax Credit is one of the many expiring tax provisions that Congress takes up every year or two. This particular tax credit was last considered as a part of the compromise tax deal agreed to in December and is set to expire at the end of 2011. Simply inserting the phrase "and tribal governments" could rectify this inequity.

The Chickasaw Nation is struggling to be environmentally responsible, sensitive to national security and economically innovative in its energy policy but has been frustrated by national regulations affecting market driven opportunities.

A sound energy policy is one that is:
1. Coherent and viable (no nonsense)
2. Sustainable
3. Timely can be applied here and now
4. Should help not harm the national economy and the environment

We believe that, at a micro level in the Chickasaw Nation that our policy of using clean burning natural gas meets these criteria and we are implementing it with great success that can be magnified with the implementation of these suggested changes in tax and regulatory controls. It can be of greater value at a national level using the same criteria if the regulatory obstacles are mitigated.

With this in mind, Mr. Chairman, I would like to commend Congressman Boren for his leadership last year in promoting the Natural Gas Act—which would have provided federal incentives for; natural gas vehicle purchase—both dedicated and bi-fuel; purchasing of natural gas fuel; and installing CNG fueling stations. It is my understanding that a similar NAT GAS Act will be introduced in the House shortly, which would also allow Indian tribes to be eligible for these incentives and we will be very supportive of that legislation.

In closing let me point out that almost half of our oil consumption goes for on-road transportation purposes, and last year, we imported about 60% of all the petro-leum we used. If we only substituted natural gas for half of that use, we would cut our oil imports by two thirds. Natural gas is the only available option that could actually accomplish this. This is not a speculative policy as 30% of European autos are now fueled by CNG and these countries are importers of the fuel. Most impor-tantly for today's hearing, many tribal areas in the US have extensive deposits of natural gas, and this energy policy will provide economic opportunities in Indian Country by increasing demand for natural gas.

———

Mr. YOUNG. Thank you very much. Mr. Connolly.

STATEMENT OF MICHAEL CONNOLLY, PRESIDENT, LAGUNA RESOURCES SERVICES, INCORPORATED

Mr. CONNOLLY. Good afternoon, Mr. Chairman, and Members of the Subcommittee. I want to thank you for the opportunity to appear here today. My name is Michael Connolly. I am a member of the Campo Band of Mission Indians in San Diego County.

I have served as an elected representative for the Band for over 17 years, 17 of the past 25 years. I am an engineer with over 15 years working on both Indian and non-Indian projects in the environmental and energy fields.

As you have heard today, the opportunities for energy contributions to the national portfolio are substantial. My particular exper-tise has been in the development of wind energy projects, which will be the focus of my comments today.

As you know, Indian lands represent five percent of the United States land base, while holding the potential of 10 percent of the renewable resources. It is in the interests of Indian Country and the Nation as a whole, that these resources be harnessed.

When they are harnessed, significant benefit will be produced in some cases for some of the most impoverished communities in the country, while simultaneously helping to diversify the United States energy portfolio.

I am going to outline some of the basic problems that I have en-countered over the last few years in moving into the development of commercial-scale wind energy projects. As you are all no doubt aware, there has been a recurring theme of resource extraction or use in Indian Country that provided very little or no economic gain to tribal communities over time.

That painful legacy has only begun to change over the last 30 years. Resources were often taken from Indian lands for royalty payments that were deemed fair by Federal officials, who had little stake in the welfare of the community.

The end result of decades of this treatment is that tribes, as they have moved forward into resource development, have developed a fundamental mistrust of these passive types of deals, and they want to be owners, and they want to have a part of the project.

They don't want to simply turn it over to somebody from outside the community to run and operate for them. This has become a central criterion, and in some cases, they actually want a majority stake in any type of energy project that develops on the reservation.

Tribes are also governments, and like any thoughtful, reasonable government, they want to realize the full economic potential of a project that comes on their land. They have to look not only to the project and the value of the project in the role of an owner who is leasing their property, but also if they do want to buy into the project, then they are also entering into a relationship as a developer.

And then on top of that, as a government, they have to look at the services that they need to provide to their people as a government, not only as to their members, but also to the residents, and visitors, and workers who operate on their tribal lands.

So when tribes look at participating in a wind energy project as a developer, they face a substantial hurdle, in that the government incentives for these types of projects are based on Production Tax Credits, Investment Tax Credits, and Accelerated Depreciation.

As governments, they are not eligible to use that, and so they are penalized. The more tribal ownership you have in one of these projects, the less benefit you are going to get from the tax credits and from the depreciation.

In some cases that is over 50 percent of the value of the project, and in many cases, this is enough to kill it. Tribes, as governments, are also looking at the tax revenues that come off of these projects. And there it varies considerably across the country, but there are varying levels of intrusion from State and local governments on to reservation projects. Consider a 200 megawatt project on tribal lands. This could generate over 15 million dollars in sales tax right up front, which in some States, 100 percent of that goes to the States, and in some States, they do share that revenue back with the tribes.

A one percent property tax could exceed 33 million dollars in value over a 20 year period for the project, and there are hundreds of millions of dollars in corporate and individual taxable income that occurs over the 20 year project life.

So the reality is that this intrusion of State and local tax authorities on to tribal projects has resulted in part or all of the potential tribal revenue being siphoned off into State and local coffers.

The result of this taxation is that many projects not only lose the government revenue that they should be getting to provide governmental services on their lands, but some tribes just choose not to develop the projects because of that.

My time is getting short here. Just to give you a real quick example here. For my Tribe, the Campo Band, we developed a 50 megawatt project, and we came very close to not even doing it because of the tax issues that were involved.

Not only did we have to look at tens of millions of dollars being siphoned off to other jurisdictions who were providing no services to the project area, but we also had to look at the property tax generation that was coming off the project going into the county, while we were the ones that were paying for the governmental services that were being provided.

So in effect what we ended up seeing in our community was that the off-reservation governmental jurisdictions were actually making more than what we ended up getting from the royalty on the project.

Fortunately, we only did a small project, and it was a way for us to get our foot in the door, but I think that these types of issues are one of the reasons why there has only been on commercial scale wind energy project in Indian Country over the last six years. Thank you.

[The prepared statement of Mr. Connolly follows:]

Statement of Michael L. Connolly, President,
Laguna Resource Services, Inc.

Introduction

Good morning Chairman Young, Ranking Member Boren and members of the Subcommittee on Indian and Alaska Native Affairs. Thank you for the opportunity to appear before you today to discuss this critically important topic for our nation as a whole and Indian Country in particular.

By way of introduction, I am a member of the Campo Band of Mission Indians in San Diego County (Campo Band). I served as an elected representative of the tribe for over 17 years. I am an engineer and for over 15 years have worked both on Indian and non-Indian projects as an environmental and energy consultant. This experience has given me the opportunity to recognize the legal, regulatory and institutional hurdles Indian tribes face in trying to develop their natural resources and improve the standards of living of their members.

My testimony today is to highlight the great potential for renewable energy development in Indian Country. As you know, Indian lands represent 5% of the U.S. land base, while holding the potential of 10% of the renewable resources. It is in the interest of Indian Country and the nation that these resources be harnessed. When they are harnessed significant benefit will be produced for some of our most impoverished communities, while simultaneously helping to diversify the energy portfolio of the United States.

In the following paragraphs, I will outline some of the basic problems that hinder the development of renewable energy resources in Indian tribal communities and make what I hope you will agree are reasonable recommendations to overcome these problems.

Background

For Indian tribal communities, the recurring theme of resource extraction or use with little or no economic gain to the tribal community is a painful legacy that has only begun to change in the last 30 years. Resources were taken from Indian lands for a royalty payment that often was often deemed "fair" by Federal officials who had little stake in the welfare of the community. These raw resources then went to off-reservation locations where they were transformed into valuable products sold into the commercial markets. The end result of decades of such treatment is a fundamental mistrust of "passive" energy deals which simply extract resources and fail to invest in the long-term health of tribal economies.

In recent years, many Indian tribes have made tribal ownership a central criterion for any large-scale development on their tribal lands.

Tribes, like any thoughtful and reasonable government, want to ensure that the full benefit of economic development is maximized for their citizens and the community as a whole. As such, the dual role of tribes as owners and potential developers must be viewed in terms of the obligation of tribal governments to provide services like law enforcement, education, elder care, emergency services, environmental protection and the like to their members, residents, visitors and employees within the reservation.

Tribes, as *owners,* face a substantial hurdle in that governments are unable to take advantage of incentives such as the production/investment tax credits and accelerated depreciation that can represent over 50% of the value of a commercial scale wind or solar project. Not only can the unavailability of these incentives make a project untenable, it almost certainly makes the tribal project uncompetitive.

Indian tribes, as *governments,* face an additional constraint in that potential tax revenues that are expected and relied on in off-reservation projects are subject to varying levels of intrusion from state and local governments for on-reservation projects. Consider the following example: a modest 200 megawatt project on tribal lands could generate over $15 million dollars in sales tax (at 6%), $33 million in property tax (at 1%) and hundreds of millions in corporate and individual taxable income over a twenty-year project life. The reality is that the intrusion of state and local tax authorities into tribal projects over the last 30 years has resulted in part, or all, of the potential tribal revenue being siphoned off into the state and local coffers.

The result of this excessive taxation of a project's revenues is not only the loss of revenue to fund governmental services on Indian lands, but the added possibility that tribes will refrain from developing their resources in the first instance.

A case in point is the Campo Band. The Campo Band was the first tribe in the nation to develop a large scale wind energy development, which was put into operation in 2005. For the Campo Band, the desire to enter the renewable energy field was balanced against the inherent economic unfairness and the uneven playing field described above. The tribe decided that a 50 megawatt wind project would give it the opportunity to enter the renewable energy field, while continuing to work to achieve a fairer system for future projects. With a potential of an additional 250 megawatts, the initial project was determined to be a conservative first step. This was a difficult decision, however, as it meant accepting the fact that tens of millions of dollars in sales tax would be collected by state and county governments, and that none would be shared with the tribe. Additionally, property taxes (currently over $300,000) generated annually by the Campo project are taken entirely by San Diego County, again with none going to the tribe. (While Congress and the Courts have made it clear that outside governing bodies have no right to directly tax tribal lands, the courts have found that the non-Indian interests in leases of tribal lands are a taxable property right. While there is nothing preventing a tribe from developing its own property tax, the specter of dual taxation often makes projects economically infeasible.) When property tax is correlated with population, the Campo members generate a higher property tax per capita than the local off-reservation community. Yet, Campo provides the fire protection, emergency medical, environmental protection and other services to the project and the local community, without benefit of any of the tax revenues it generated through on-Reservation projects.

Potential Remedies

Against the backdrop of being penalized as both a developer and as a government, tribes are pressured into a passive lease holder relationship with an outside developer, the relationship that offers the lowest value for the tribal community and represents, sadly, a repeat of the historical method of resource removal and exploitation that tribes have fought so hard to overcome. (Typically, because of limited revenue, on–reservation projects have been developed by outside third party non-Indian developers. Because of federal restrictions on agreements that encumber Indian lands third-party development usually requires the transfer of a leasehold interest to the developer. Approval of such leasee requires extensive bureaucratic review, including but not limited to review under the National Environmental Policy Act (NEPA), that can actually take years.)

A level playing field would enable tribes to benefit from the dual roles of developer and government. The American Recovery and Reinvestment Act, (ARRA) temporarily corrected a long-standing disparity in tribal access to capital at more favorable rates by authorizing tribes to issue tax exempt bonds to finance economic development projects. This is the kind of reform that is enormously beneficial and should be made permanent.

Federal legislation to authorize the transferability of tax credits and depreciation allowances from Indian tribes (non-taxable entities) to private entities (Federal taxpayers) will further open the door for tribes to invest as project developers, without any loss to the Federal treasury.

Federal support for tribes in their roles as governments would be bolstered by requiring that state and local property and sales taxes be justified based on governmental services provided to the project located on tribal lands.

At the state level, tribes must work with the state legislatures to push for an equitable share of tax revenues generated from jobs and businesses with operations on tribal lands.

An equally important aspect of renewable energy development is access to the transmission and distribution systems. In many parts of the country, the national energy distribution system was not engineered with tribal access in mind. As a result, tribes often find themselves at a competitive disadvantage in relation to projects sited on state or federal lands, offering lower cost access to the distribution infrastructure. Changes to the distribution priorities through reserved set-asides for tribal energy projects, or the use of feed-in tariffs, could contribute to a more equitable playing field.

In conclusion, Mr. Chairman, while I have focused on a handful of the major economic constraints to realizing the full commercial potential of wind and solar energy projects in Indian Country, there are many other constraints that prevent tribes from realizing their resource potential. These include access to technical assistance, funds for initial feasibility studies, resource inventories, assessments, and training. Additional impediments are the secretarial leasing review and approval process which is lengthy and costly, the uneconomic appraisal requirements, and the time cost of complying with the NEPA.

I understand the Subcommittee will be preparing the legislation to reform or correct these and other problems and I urge you to consider the observations and recommendations of the National Congress of American Indians which has an ongoing effort to identify and work with Congress and the Executive Branch to address these constraints.

Making these simple, but significant, changes will help renewable energy projects to flourish in Indian Country and ultimately, contribute a significant element of the national portfolio.

I would be happy to answer any questions you have at this point.

Thank You.

––––––––

Mr. YOUNG. Thank you, and if I could make a suggestion. As I told the last panel, you give me the exact examples of how that can be rectified. You write it out on what you run into, and how it can be done. Is it Myore, or what is your name, Manuel?

Mr. MYORE. Manuel Myore.

Mr. YOUNG. On most panels, I heard no—or no one has mentioned the fact that do you think that you could handle the leasing and the whole program, instead of going through the Federal agencies, could you do it?

Mr. MYORE. I believe we can. At the Ute Tribe Energy and Minerals Department, we mostly handle basically everything that is from the APDs, to the surveys. We have operators doing their own environmental analysis to present with the APD applications.

But the only problem that we have there is the lack of staffing on the bureau who oversees, and looks, and reviews the environmental assessments.

Mr. YOUNG. But what I am leading up to is that I don't want the BIA to being a deterrent. Could you do that assessment, or does there have to be another assessment on the outside?

Why do we have to have the BIA involved in this to begin with? I mean, that is all that I am hearing, and that is sort of a constant theme, is that the EPA, the BIA, the 49 different steps, why does that have to be there?

Is there any reason for them to be doing what they are doing? There is no way that we are going to raise the BIA budget to the degree for this type of thing, because they are not producing four permits you said, and if needed, about 400?

Mr. MYORE. We do about—we are going to be looking at 400 or 500 APD permits, but we are only getting four permits per month.

Mr. YOUNG. And that is what I am saying, because the BIA is not doing them, correct?

Mr. MYORE. Exactly.

Mr. YOUNG. So why can't you guys do it?

Mr. MYORE. I believe we can. I mean, we just need to get out from under the thumb of the Federal Government.

Mr. YOUNG. And that is what I want to do, and that is the whole intent of this deal. We are about ready to get out of time, and so Mr. Boren, you can ask your next question.

Who has got that cell phone on? That is a good way to get in real trouble with me over time. I hate those things.

Mr. BOREN. I had better turn my cell phone off, Mr. Chairman. Let me make sure. Thank you again for being here, for all of you being here today. We talked a little bit about—Mr. McCaleb talked a little bit about the Natural Gas Act, which was not only introduced in the last Congress, but it has been introduced in the last couple of Congresses.

We have had over a hundred cosponsors, nearly 200 cosponsors, bipartisan, Democrats and Republicans. The first one that was introduced actually even had Rahm Emanuel, and in the Senate, Orin Hatch and Bob Menendez introduced a Senate companion bill.

Let me ask you a little bit about the Natural Gas Act and how it would impact the Chickasaw Nation. If the bill were to pass, and we will be reintroducing this legislation with Congressman Sullivan and others, but if it were to pass, how would that influence the Chickasaw Nation's expansion for these filling stations?

How much more investment would occur for you all if the bill were to pass?

Mr. McCALEB. I think that if the bill is passed—well, each station costs us about $500,000. The recovery on that is fairly slow until you get more CNG cars on the road. So one of the things the bill would do, as introduced in the last Congress, is help us with the excise tax credit at 50 cents per gallon for every gallon we would pump. That would be very helpful to defer our capital costs.

It would make the case for tax credits for bi-fuel cars, as well as CNG dedicated cars. That means that there are going to be more cars on the road, and more fuel consumed, and therefore our capital costs are retired faster.

And, third, we are hopeful that the EPA certification process as provided in your bill before would have been expedited, and I think that is a huge deterrent for the increase in the number of CNG vehicles on the road.

So I think the bill would be very helpful, and I think that it would increase the market, and therefore, reduce our capital costs. We are very supportive of those principles.

Mr. BOREN. A follow-up question on that. You mentioned the $10,000 cost for changing some of these vehicles over. Can you kind of explain the EPA's role in the after-market conversion process?

And what could be done to lessen the burden to the vehicle owner? How can we get that cost down other than just——

Mr. McCALEB. Well, we were told from our suppliers that original equipment manufacturing, which is the after-market converters, in Ocarta, Oklahoma, that the EPA requires that each year, each make, each model, be recertified.

If you had had that same make certified in the previous year, even in the subsequent year, you had to get it recertified, even though it is the same engine, the same car, the same model, the same everything.

Well, the cost of that, it is my understanding, is somewhere between $150,000 to $300,000. I think that we can all appreciate the cost implications of that. So that streamlining and duplication of effort on certification is unnecessary and costly.

Mr. BOREN. Well, I thank you for your responses. I think, Mr. Chairman, as we come up with this big massive bill, and obviously I have stand-alone legislation with the Natural Gas Act, but some of these things that we have learned from the Chickasaw Nation, hopefully we can incorporate it in a much larger bill.

Mr. YOUNG. The Gentleman brings a good point. Why in the world if they want clean air, why would it be a requirement to re-certify an automobile that burns natural gas?

I have never understood that. You know what I want to do? Have you ever seen these ads that they have on television now for anxiety, and for colds, and all this other stuff? Thousands of pharmaceutical ads for Viagra, Cialis, and all of that sort of thing?

I want them to really take those drug companies and start concentrating on developing a logic pill, and every legislature, and everybody in government has to take one logic pill a day, and we would really be in good shape, because there is no logic in this.

Now, one question. The car that you were talking about, Neal, it would have to have two tanks, right? One for regular gas and one for natural gas?

Mr. MCCALEB. This is a standard Impala, Chevy Impala, and then you get it in the aftermarket, and they would install a natural gas tank. So, you can run on either fuel. In fact, it actually starts on regular fuel, and then it switches over to natural gas automatically.

Mr. YOUNG. Well, I was just curious about how you are going to fill a gas tank with natural gas.

Mr. BOREN. I yield back.

Mr. YOUNG. Mr. Kildee.

Mr. KILDEE. Thank you very much, Mr. Chairman. Ms. Cuch, you said that in 2005 the Tribe reached agreement with SITLA that SITLA would relinquish certain mineral interests within the boundaries of the reservation.

In turn, the Tribe would deal with SITLA in making similar arrangements. You called that a win-win situation, and an agreement apparently has been reached with SITLA. That has been pending before the Department of the Interior for quite some time now, since 2006, and the Department of the Interior says they don't have the legal authority to approve that.

Now, it seems to me that if they don't have the legal authority, and I doubt that they don't have it, that Congress should give them the legal authority to make such agreements. When two representatives of sovereignties come together and agree on something, then the BIA or the Department of the Interior should be authorized to approve that, if indeed approval is needed. Would you care to comment on that?

Ms. CUCH. Yes, thank you for the question. This exchange, and I guess it is called the Land Exchange, or SITLA, or the school sections within the exterior boundaries of the reservation, and it has been on the table for years.

But as stated the State of Utah has agreed to make that exchange, and the only problem is that the Department of the Interior has said that they lack the authority to make this exchange, to approve it, and that is where it is at now.

But Congressman Matheson did introduce H.R. 1053, and it is cosponsored by Representative Rob Bishop of Utah. This will take care of that hopefully, where this exchange will be done.

And as I stated, it has been on the table for years. I can remember this going back when I was first on the tribal council back in 1969 or 1970. This was talked about then, this land exchange.

And so it has been on the books, I guess you could say, throughout the years by previous council members. Some are gone now. So this is a dream that has been there. Hopefully Mr. Young, Mr. Boren, and the rest of the Committee support Jim Matheson's bill, and this will make that dream come true by making that exchange, and making it one.

It is a primitive area, and if you take that out and it will be a solid tribal area, both surface and subsurface. But that exchange has been agreed to, except that the Department of the Interior has said they don't have the authority.

So if you can support Jim Matheson's bill, then that would take care of it.

Mr. KILDEE. I think that the two sovereignties, and the State out there, and the SITLA, which is an agency of the State, and the Tribe, two sovereigns, have agreed, and the Department of the Interior should get out of the way really.

But I will at your suggestion cosponsor Mr. Matheson and Mr. Bishop's bill. That is a good bill because it is a bipartisan bill, and to make sure that if the Department of the Interior lacks or does not even know its own authority, that we make it clear that they have that authority.

I think that you have done a good job in negotiating with the State agency and in achieving what you have achieved, and I would support that. I appreciate your testimony. It was very good. I read part of it this morning, and I found it very revealing, and I appreciate it. I yield back, Mr. Chairman.

Ms. CUCH. OK. Thank you.

Mr. YOUNG. The good lady from Hawaii.

Ms. HANABUSA. Thank you, Mr. Chairman. Thank you to all of our witnesses. My questions are for Mr. Connolly. Mr. Connolly, I found the references in your testimony about the dual role of developer and government, and how somehow in that process that it is a disincentive for the Tribes to actually go forward with development of renewable energy.

But before I go there, you did mention that the AR temporarily corrected a longstanding problem of accessibility to capital, and you wanted it to become permanent. Can you expand on that for me so that I can understand what you were referencing?

Mr. CONNOLLY. The ability of Tribal governments to use tax exempt bonds, they were restricted since the 1980s to only essential governmental services, and that was narrowly defined as basically drinking water systems, and sewerage systems, and things like that, that served primarily a tribal population.

So tribes were not able to use those types of bonds for economic development, and in the ARA, that was expanded so that tribes could use it for any type of economic development, except for gaming.

And the number of tribes that signed up for the bonds, both times with Treasury, they reserved a hundred percent, and so the need is out there in Indian Country for that type of access to capital.

Ms. HANABUSA. Did your Tribe, the Campo Tribe, also sign up for bonds?

Mr. CONNOLLY. Yes, for another wind project that the tribe is looking at doing, and there was also an expansion of Investment Tax Credits to allow them to be used in wind energy, which in the past, they were only used for solar.

And under the ARA, you could also get a grant up front for the projected tax credits that you would get in the future, and that is a very good instrument to allow tribes to try to buy into part of the project with their tax credits.

Ms. HANABUSA. One of the other statements that you made that I found troubling is that you said that the non-tribal governmental entities make more money than the tribal governmental entities do because of all of the different taxes that are just sort of taken out of the system, because you are unable to take advantage of the tax credits, and the accelerated depreciation. Did I recall you correctly on what you said?

Mr. CONNOLLY. Yes, there are kind of two things there. The other jurisdictions are able to tax from the tribal jurisdiction, and it varies. Some tribes have worked out arrangements with the States they live in, and some of the States repatriate a part of the tax base back to the Tribes.

In some cases, and I think in the State of Utah, they allow the Navajo Nation property tax to displace Utah property tax. In others, they have negotiated agreements where they share part of the possessory interest tax back with the Tribes.

That is the governmental side of it, and what we have in California, we don't have a lot of political clout. California has more Indians than any other State in the country, but as a percentage of the population, we are so tiny that it is very difficult for us to change things legislatively in the State.

We have 100 percent of the property tax, sales tax, that comes off the reservation and goes to the State and county, and zero is shared back with the tribal government, regardless of the level of tribal services that are provided.

The other part of it is the Tribe as a developer. You know, many Tribes want to be the developer because they don't want to be a passive lessee to outside parties to come and work on the reservation.

So they either want to raise the capital, or in some cases, they have tribal funds that they want to invest, but because over half of the project is based on the tax credits and the accelerated depreciation, that ownership means that they lose that.

So one of the proposals that—I think it was actually proposed in legislation that did not get passed, but it was to allow transferability of the Production Tax Credit and Accelerated Depreciation.

So that way when a Tribe could enter into a partnership, where maybe they owned 51 percent, and the private developers owned 49 percent, and they could transfer those tax incentives to the private developer in return for a larger share of the revenue stream. That way the project, as a whole, would be able to realize the full benefit, and the cost to the Treasury would be zero in that case.

Ms. HANABUSA. OK. Thank you. Look at Act 221 in Hawaii. It generated a lot of money. Thank you.

Mr. CONNOLLY. Thank you.

Ms. HANABUSA. Thank you, Mr. Chairman.

Mr. YOUNG. Mr. Pallone.

Mr. PALLONE. Thank you. I just wanted the Chairman to know that the reason that I was absent had nothing to do with the government. It was totally personal. I wanted to ask Mr. Connolly that you have used the Campo Band as an example of State and county governments taxing Indian energy projects.

And I believe that State and local governments have no authority to tax tribal lands, and in fact, it may be unconstitutional. But I know that this problem has been complicated in some instances because of the limbo that many Indian lands now stand due to the Carcieri decision.

Could you elaborate on your experience, and give us some recommendations on how this might be prevented in the future?

Mr. CONNOLLY. I understand that there has been some work with the National Congress of American Indians to see if there might be a solution administratively, and that if there are improvements on tribal land that they can be considered part of the land, and therefore not taxable by the State or county.

These projects have such a huge capital investment that the property tax that they generate is just tremendous, and the impacts to the off-reservation community are almost nothing.

In our case, putting in a 50 megawatt project is generating over $300,000 in property tax for Campo. If you divide that by the number of tribal members on the reservation, we are generating more property tax per capita than the non-Indians who live next to us off-reservation, and yet they are getting all the governmental services from the county.

We have to pay for the fire protection, and for security, for roads, for environmental. All of those things, we have to dedicate out of our revenue stream to pay for that because our tax base is being siphoned off.

Mr. PALLONE. I understand and I agree with you, and the reason that I brought this up is because NCAI and some of the other groups brought it to my attention, and so I know that it is a problem.

But in your testimony, you also noted that as owners, Tribes face substantial hurdles in taking advantage of incentives, such as the Production and Investment Tax Credits, and Accelerated Depreciation.

Can you just elaborate on what your experience has been, and in your experience what has created these hurdles, and any thoughts that you may have on how to ensure that Tribes can develop their resources and pursue new projects without conceding control over them?

Mr. CONNOLLY. I did discuss that a little bit when I think you were out of the room, but allowing the transferability of the Production Tax Credit or Accelerated Depreciation would go a long way toward resolving that.

And the situation that we are in right now in Indian Country is that we are really kind of being pushed in the direction of being just a passive leaseholder, because if we invest, then we are going to be penalized by not having access to the tax credits.

But then if we don't, then the local jurisdictions get to siphon off the revenue stream that comes from it, because it is being owned by non-members. So it is really a tough position to be in.

If we had the transferability, I think what we have with the Investment Tax Credit, and the ability to get the grant of the credit up front, I think is a tremendous tool that can help tribes there again to buy in and have an ownership in the facility.

But even there, they are still going to have to have an official owner who is a taxable entity in order to realize that up front grant. So it puts tribes in this position of having to bring in somebody to kind of basically be the legal titleholder for a period of time until they can justify the exemptions, or the credits, and then try to transfer after that time.

And, of course, the more people that you have in your deal, everybody is taking their cut, and it ends up reducing the profitability of the project.

Mr. PALLONE. Did you talk about expanding the Work Opportunity Tax Credit to Native Americans? Did you already talk about that?

Mr. CONNOLLY. No, I didn't.

Mr. PALLONE. Because that was one of the other things that I have heard, is that that would remove barriers to employment and encourage businesses to hire your members.

Mr. CONNOLLY. I think in the first panel, I think one of the speakers on that mentioned that.

Mr. PALLONE. OK. I know that the Chairman is talking about a comprehensive bill in this regard, and so I am sure that you are going to address a lot of these things. But I appreciate your responses, and thank you, Mr. Chairman.

Mr. YOUNG. I thank the Gentleman, and the same to this panel here. I may have some other questions, but I wanted to make the comment that we are going to write a bill, and I need your suggestions on how you think in your arena how it can be improved.

The challenge that we are going to have is—and this panel has been talking about taxes quite a bit, and the last one did, too. When we write this bill, and unless I get the blessing from the leadership, we would have to write a bill that would go to Ways and Means.

And that is not the friendliest committee right now. So we are going to maybe have to have two separate bills, and one would solve the tax part of it so that we can send it over there, and so they can move it, and keep the rest of it together.

I have never understood one thing. A reservation is a Nation; is that not correct? Is that correct? It is a sovereign Nation?

Mr. CONNOLLY. Well, sovereignty can exist without a reservation.

Mr. YOUNG. OK. But what I am saying is that where in the world did they get the idea that they can tax an improvement on an reservation?

Mr. CONNOLLY. It has been the result of a lot of court cases, some very significant ones, especially in the last 20 or 30 years that have allowed the States this intrusion into the Tribal tax basis.

Mr. YOUNG. But again though that could be changed couldn't it? I would like to stir the pot up. That would be fine.

Mr. CONNOLLY. I would like to see it addressed, and I would like to see the pot stirred—if for no other reason than to let people understand that there is tax coming off of reservation lands.

There are so many people in this Nation who think that no taxes come from reservation lands, or that Indians are not taxed, and that is just not the case. As I explained in our case, we are generating a higher share of tax than the people who live off-reservation.

And in return we are getting far, far less in the services that a government should be providing for those taxes. So I would like people just to know that, whether it went anywhere or not, just to educate people on the fact that this is occurring in Indian Country.

Mr. YOUNG. All right. Has anybody got any other questions?

Mr. BOREN. Just one.

Mr. YOUNG. Go ahead.

Mr. BOREN. Back to Secretary McCaleb. You know, having not only the Chickasaw Nation perspective, but the BIA perspective, we talked a lot about streamlining the process, and about improving—you know, whether it is oil and gas leasing, or whatever it may be, with the BIA.

And I know that the BIA currently is involved in revising some of its leasing regulations right now. Are you optimistic that having your experience, do you see us doing this administratively before we get into some of this stuff?

Will Mr. Echo Hawk have some successes, or do you see something like that coming about?

Mr. MCCALEB. My candid opinion is no. BIA clings tenaciously to the idea that anything that has to do with the alienation of title to land or assets of a sovereign tribe is a trust responsibility and cannot be delegated. That is the problem.

Mr. BOREN. Great, and that is the response that I thought.

Mr. YOUNG. And that is what I am seeking to do in this legislation.

Mr. MCCALEB. Excellent.

Mr. YOUNG. Because they have become a stagnated agency over the years, and they are not allowing the tribes to progress, and they will deny that. And I don't blame Mr. Echo Hawk. This is because they are at the bottom of that barrel.

They have the Secretary, and you have the Park Service, and you have the Fish and Wildlife, and you have the BLM, and you have the Minerals Management, and way down here, Mr. Secretary, is you, and you have to go through all of that nonsense to get to the Secretary himself.

And you have always had to take the back end of that bus, and like I said, I have been through all kinds of Secretaries, and BIA chiefs, and I just want to change that, where if they can't do the job, then we have to write legislation that allows for the streamlining of progress to let you people get on your feet.

And by the way, I am going to in this bill—it is not just going to be gas and oil, but it is going to be wind power, and hydro, and all those energy sources. I think that is crucially important.

We are about ready to have a vote, and I want to thank you all for your testimony, and keep in contact with the Committee. This is a bipartisan committee, and it works very closely together, and hopefully you will help us write a pretty good piece of legislation in the realm of energy and all the rest that we hope to put in there, and call it the Empowerment Act.

With that, thank you ladies and gentlemen, this meeting is adjourned.

[Whereupon, at 2:25 p.m., the Subcommittee was adjourned.]

[Additional material submitted for the record follows:]

[A letter submitted for the record by the Arctic Slope Regional Corporation follows:]

Anchorage Office • 3900 C Street • Suite 801 • Anchorage • Alaska 99503-5963 • (907) 339-6000 • FAX (907) 339-6028 • 1 (800) 770-2772

arctic slope
regional corporation

Public Comments Processing
Subcommittee on Indian and Alaska Native Affairs
Committee on Natural Resources
U.S. House of Representatives
1337 Longworth Building

April 15, 2011

Filed electronically at http://www.regulations.gov

> Re: Comments on Oversight Hearing on "Tribal development of energy resources and the creation of energy jobs on Indian lands" held by the Subcommittee on Indian and Alaska Native Affairs and House Committee on Natural Resources (April 1, 2011)

Dear Chairman Young:

Arctic Slope Regional Corporation ("ASRC"), an Alaska Native Regional Corporation created at the direction of Congress pursuant to the Alaska Native Claims Settlement Act of 1971[1], respectfully submits the following comments in connection with the above-referenced Oversight Hearing (the "Hearing") held by the Subcommittee on Indian and Alaska Native Affairs, part of the House Committee on Natural Resources (the "Committee"). At the Hearing, stakeholders discussed the regulatory obstacles Native Americans face in developing Native-owned lands containing valuable energy resources. We submit these comments so that the Committee can better understand how this excessive regulation inhibits energy resource development in the North Slope region of Alaska to the detriment of the region's Iñupiat Eskimo communities.

As the largest Alaskan-owned company, a landowner and lessor of subsurface rights in the North Slope, a business partner for oil, gas and coal companies working in the region, and a public voice for our 11,000 Iñupiat Eskimo shareholders, ASRC has a unique perspective to contribute to the debate. Our five major lines of business are energy support services, petroleum refining and marketing, government services, construction, and resource development. Any changes in the regulatory climate have a significant impact on our family of companies and the communities within which we do business.

There are several overreaching federal policies that aim to lock up Alaska's North Slope from oil, gas and coal development, or that have a chilling effect on business investment opportunities in the Arctic. North Slope landowners face overlapping regulatory pressure from multiple federal agencies, including the Department of the Interior ("DOI"), the Environmental Protection Agency, the National Marine Fisheries Service and the National Oceanic and Atmospheric Administration. As you know, the DOI, using the Endangered Species Act ("ESA"), recently set aside an area larger than the state of California

---

[1] See 43 U.S.C. § 1606.

as Critical Habitat for polar bears—potentially the largest ever Critical Habitat designation in the history of the ESA. The DOI is considering Critical Habitat designation for several other species that could lead to overlapping designations. The DOI also plans to set aside additional areas on the North Slope that will cover millions of acres both on- and off-shore. Significant efforts are underway to designate vast areas of our homeland as Wild Lands within the National Petroleum Reserve-Alaska. The Arctic National Wildlife Refuge is under consideration to receive National Monument or Wilderness status designation. The crushing cumulative effect of these multiple federal designations is to curtail the use and development of lands inhabited by the Iñupiat for thousands of years.

With most prospective areas on-shore either off-limits or at risk of becoming off-limits, we are unable to offset the dramatic production decline of the existing oilfields. This decline is not just a lingering tail of decreasing production, but will become a "brick wall" when the pipeline reaches its mechanical limits and is unable to move production. Decline in production equates to a decline to the well-being of our shareholders who live in the North Slope villages. There is no other economy in our region. Our shareholders ask, how will our grandchildren clear snow from our roads, maintain our schools, and operate the real-world infrastructure that makes our villages safe and viable into the future?

This concerns ASRC, and should concern all lawmakers. ASRC and, in general, the people of the North Slope have a heightened concern for the environmental effects of oil, gas and coal exploration and development. The animals that our shareholders depend upon for food and culture migrate over large ranges on the land and in the ocean. Our eyes are open regarding on- and off-shore development of our lands: we know there are risks and we believe that they can be mitigated appropriately. We face a daily onslaught of new federal programs, initiatives and management plans to the point that we are inundated with the need to respond. The federal government's approach will lead to the extinction of our communities on the North Slope and a reduction in the valuable energy resources available from American sources, all under the auspices of protecting areas and species that science says do not need protections at this time.

We appreciate the opportunity to provide these comments and ask that the Committee members support limits on federal regulation of our lands to protect the future of the Iñupiat life and the economy of the North Slope.

Sincerely,
ARCTIC SLOPE REGIONAL CORPORATION

Tara M. Sweeney
Senior Vice President
External Affairs

[The prepared statement of Mr. Markey follows:]

Statement of The Honorable Edward J. Markey, a Representative in Congress from the State of Massachusetts

I've been on the Natural Resources Committee for my entire 36 years in Congress but I have not had much opportunity to work with the Tribes.

While I may be new to Indian issues, I'm not new to energy issues. Tribes are already making important contribution to America's energy supply. I look forward to working with you on ways to use energy development to create economic opportunities for tribes, especially with the vast renewable resources that exist on tribal lands. The Bureau of Indian Affairs has indicated to me that there are millions of megawatts of potential energy from wind, solar, geothermal and biomass in Indian country. Yet so far there is just one utility-scale wind project on the Campo Band's land in southern California. That needs to change.

While tribal natural resources have provided crucial economic development to some tribes, we can't ignore the potential negative impacts as well. The Navajos are still suffering from the impact of uranium mining during World War II. The Crow have lost some their ancestral lands to the building of a dam. I look forward to working with you to pursue energy development that is both good for your economic development and good for the health of your people and your lands.

○